I loved this book!
You will, too.

DAVID STEVENS, MD, MA (ETHICS)
CEO, CHRISTIAN MEDICAL & DENTAL ASSOCIATIONS

RESOLVE

How Faith Becomes Sight

ELAINE LEONG ENG, MD

RESOLVE
How Faith Becomes Sight
by Elaine Leong Eng, MD
Copyright© 2016, Elaine Leong Eng, MD

Published by:
Healthy Life Press • 6700 Wadsworth Blvd • Arvada, CO 80003
www.healthylifepress.com • info@healthylifepress.com

Designer: Judy Johnson
Printed in the United States of America

No part of this publication may be reproduced, stored in a retrieval system, or transmitted in any form or by any means—for example, electronic, photocopy, recording—without the prior written permission of the author, except for brief quotations in printed reviews.

Library of Congress Cataloging-in-Publication Data
Eng, Elaine Leong, MD
Resolve: How Faith Becomes Sight

ISBN 978-1-939267-45-0
1. Religion / Christian Life / Inspirational; 2. Religion / Christianity / Counseling

All Scripture quotations, unless otherwise indicated, are taken from The Holy Bible, New International Version® NIV®, Copyright © 1973, 1978, 1984, 2011 by Biblica, Inc.® Used by permission. All rights reserved worldwide. Scripture references marked NASB are taken from the New American Standard Bible. Copyright © 1960, 1962, 1963, 1968, 1971, 1972, 1973, 1975, 1977 by the Lockman Foundation. Used by permission. Scripture references marked KJV are from the King James Version. Scriptures marked NKJV are from the New King James Version, Copyright © 1982 by Thomas Nelson. Scriptures marked NLT are from the Holy Bible, New Living Translation, Copyright © 1996, 2004, 2007 by Tyndale House Publishers.

Capitalization of pronouns related to deity follows *The Christian Writer's Manual of Style* (Grand Rapids: Zondervan, 2004). In biblical quotes, capitalization of pronoun related to deity follows the translation used in that passage.

The opinions expressed in this book are those of the author, and may or may not represent the official views of Healthy Life Press or its other authors.
Some identities have been disguised to protect the privacy of individuals involved.

Most Healthy Life Press resources are available wherever books are sold. Distribution is primarily through www.Amazon.com, www.deepershopping.com, and www.healthylifepress.com. Multiple copy discounts available directly from Healthy Life Press. Wholesale distribution is through www.SpringArbor.com (a division of www.IngramContent.com.) Our ePublications are available through www.healthylifepress.com, www.Amazon.com (Kindle), www.BNcom (Nook), and for all eBook readers through www.deepershopping.com. Resources ordered directly from the publisher receive free shipping. For information on our products, or how to publish with us, e-mail: info@healthylifepress.com.

Photo of the author on the back cover is courtesy of Andres Valenzuela Photography:
www.andresvalenzuela.com.
Front cover photo credit: Biletskiy | Dreamstime.com

Dedication

This book is lovingly dedicated to Emanuel.

Acknowledgements

Many thanks to Helen Rapoza who told me this book would happen, David Biebel who made it happen, and my family, friends, students, collaborators, and innumerable kind individuals. You have provided a helping hand and valuable vision to assist in guiding me from one step to the next in all these endeavors. I am truly humbled and grateful for such a rich supply of love and providence.

Table of Contents

Publisher's Preface

Foreword

Introduction   1

Chapter 1: Straining for the Goal   9

Chapter 2: Hawaiian Winds   17

Chapter 3: Mind the Gap   31

Chapter 4: The Willow in Japan   51

Chapter 5: Resolve in Real Time: One Doctor's Story   67

Chapter 6: Three Children of Honduras   91

Chapter 7: The Parable of Paros   99

Chapter 8: A Life Worth Living   107

Chapter 9: A Call Worth Pursuing   117

Chapter 10: Faith Vision   123

Afterword   135

Notes   139

Other Books by the Author   140

Healthy Life Press Resources   141

Publisher's Preface

In New testament days, dishonest pottery dealers would try to salvage damaged pieces of their finest, and thinnest, wares by rubbing wax into the cracks and then setting those pieces in the shadows in hopes a gullible buyer would purchase them. Discerning shoppers would take these items out into the light and hold them up to the sun, which easily displayed even a hairline fracture. Pottery that passed the test was "sun-tested," because it was "without wax." The word sincere comes from these two root words.

Beyond almost anyone I have known, Dr. Elaine Eng is "sun-tested." The very hot sun of adversity first focused its heat on her when, as a practicing Ob-gyn, in 1983 she received the diagnosis of retinitis pigmentosa, an inherited eye disease that would lead to progressive blindness.

Her response: *This so-called tragedy in my life was very much for the good. I had the chance to "see" and care for my children during their precious young years; to play with them, sing songs, teach them, feed them, and do all those wonderful mothering things that many take for granted.... My eye condition was a gift from God, affording me the privilege of time to be with my children.*

After her youngest child entered school, she retrained as a psychiatrist—the only blind woman Christian psychiatrist in the world, I venture—and during her training she helped her fellow residents to "see" more clearly the needs of their disabled patients. In other words, she fulfilled the apostle Paul's exhortation to be imitators of God: "Therefore be careful how you walk, not as unwise men but as wise, making the most of your time, because the days are evil. So then do not be foolish, but understand what the will of the Lord is" (Ephesians 5:15-17).

When we started to develop this book, we envisioned that it would be a book on resilience; you know, bouncing back. But that book refused to be written. Why? Because there are some people —specifically, people like Dr. Elaine Eng, who don't have to bounce back because they are always looking for the next practical expression of what the will of God is.

You will be challenged to embrace the same kind of thinking as you read this book, which is not just a book, but a treasure to be pondered, as in the case of Mary, the mother of Jesus, who "treasured these things, pondering them in her heart" (Luke 2:19, NASB).

Our hope is that you will not only be blessed by what you read, but that you will be inspired, even impelled by what you read, and that you will also share this message with others.

~ David B. Biebel, DMin
Publisher, Healthy Life Press

Foreword

I met a truly remarkable lady on a mission trip to Cuba a few years ago. She, along with three other doctors, joined Jeff Siegel and me on the Global Youth Baseball Federation mission team. Her name is Dr. Elaine Eng. She is a psychiatrist from New York City, who frequently goes on mission trips. By the way, I forgot to mention she is blind, but probably sees far more than the rest of us. After meeting her, I was reminded of the Helen Keller quote, "The only thing worse than being blind is having sight but no vision." Dr. Eng may be blind in the physical realm, but she certainly does not lack vision . . . or for that matter, courageous faith.

Scripture tells us, "For we walk by faith, not by sight" (2 Corinthians 5:7, KJV). These words were penned by a man who was once blind, Saul of Tarsus, who later came known as the Apostle Paul. Paul knew what it was like to be led around by others until he was healed. But the impact of those few days of blindness is seen throughout his writing. Elsewhere, he wrote, "So we fix our eyes not on what is seen, but what is unseen . . ." (2 Corinthians 4:18). I believe Dr. Eng sees the unseen very clearly, and that is why she has such vision.

She was, and is, a real inspiration to me. Going on a mission trip to any foreign country takes a certain amount of faith. Going to a communist country where the United States did not even have an embassy at the time takes another level of faith. But going to this communist country when you are blind and require assistance for the simple act of walking would seem to take a "water-walking" level of blind faith. "Vulnerable" would be the word many might use to describe her, but I think the better descriptive term would be "confident." She lives out the belief, "If God is for us, who can be against us?" (Romans 8:31).

And it was not enough for Dr. Eng to simply be in Cuba to teach and share her testimony. It was her desire to fully experience Cuba. She was the one who was insisted that we take early morning walks in the Vedado section of Havana and would ask us to describe the scenery. When we drove alongside the ocean, she wanted the bus windows open so she could smell the salty sea breeze. When she led the children's church service, she jumped and clapped her hands like a little child herself. She walked on a two-foot-wide sea wall in order to be close to the baptisms that were being performed in the ocean. She went up and down steps without a stumble. And she did all this with a smile on her face and joy in her heart. She did not let blindness or fear of the unknown/unseen keep her imprisoned in her comfort zone of the known, the familiar and the "safe."

Dr. Eng is living the abundant life. She has refused to let blindness be her excuse for not living life to the fullest or not doing everything she can in the fulfillment of the Great Commission. Helen Keller also said, "I am only one, but still I am one. I cannot do everything, but still I can do something; and because I cannot do everything, I will not refuse to do something that I can do."

While on the trip, I asked Dr. Eng if she had an area of specialization in her practice. She told me she focused on the treatment of anxiety disorders. This is the subject of one of her books: *No Worries: Spiritual & Mental Health Counseling for Anxiety*. One day while she was speaking at a house church service she told a story about her overcoming her fears and climbing a rock climbing wall. Having done a little rock climbing myself, that story really resonated with me. You see, I have a fear of heights. Well, actually, I guess it would be more accurate to say I have a fear of falling . . . and landing very hard. It is scary enough to climb a rock wall when you can see. Can you imagine climbing one when you cannot see? Our imaginations tend to magnify the danger of the unknown instead of magnifying the power and love of our great and loving God. There are three stages of fear that must be overcome in order for us to walk by faith and not by sight. I want to examine each of those stages of fear in the context of Dr. Eng's rock wall climbing adventure.

Beginning – First, Dr. Eng shared that she was able to make it to the top of the rock wall because she was willing to try. To try, we must begin. To begin to act in faith is very important. You can begin something without finishing, but it is impossible to finish without first beginning. There is a Danish proverb that states, "The highest mountain you will ever climb is the threshold." To begin something requires that we do something new; that we journey outside our comfort zone; that we change our action (or inaction). Facing a fear and not backing down is the beginning of any journey in a life of faith. Bruce Wilkinson refers to this act as facing the bully at the border and not backing down.

Continuing – Secondly, Dr. Eng said she would not give up. Somewhere along the way on any journey of faith there will come those doubts and fears which will begin to whisper in your ear that you have gone as far as you can go. Sometimes, this comes because of our fatigue. We are tired and just don't think we can go any further. Sometimes, this comes because we suddenly realize how far we have come and we are either satisfied with where we are, or we are fearful of a fall. Many individuals give up before they reach their full potential in life. The word "mediocre" literally means "half-way up the stony mountain." Dr. Eng pushed past the fear, fatigue and complacency to continue her climb, and so should we.

Completing – Finally, Dr. Eng said she listened to her instructor. It is important that we have a guide in our life—someone who has been where we want to go and has done what we want to do. Sometimes those guides come in the form of a parent, teacher, professor, instructor, mentor or pastor. Sometimes they will come in the form of a "divine appointment" with someone you have never met before. Other times, the Holy Spirit is that much-needed guide. Regardless of the source of our guidance, we all need instruction, encouragement and the wisdom needed to make it to the top.

Dr. Eng described her elation when she made it to the top, and we were all greatly encouraged. We are all capable of doing so much more than we do. We tend to let fear keep us from even attempting daring deeds. Helen Keller also spoke to this, "Security is mostly a superstition. It does not exist in nature, nor do the children of men as a whole experience it. Avoiding danger is no safer in the long run than outright exposure. Life is either a daring adventure, or nothing." To that I want to say "Amen." So, would you describe your life as a daring adventure?

As I returned from this amazing mission trip, I was thankful to a blind believer for challenging me to be bolder in my walk with the Lord and for helping me to see things more clearly than ever before.

Dr. Eng has continued to be an inspiration to me. While in Cuba, I shared with her that I served as the Chairman of a ministry to North Korean refugees called Seoul USA (this has now become Voice of the Martyrs Korea). We operated what we referred to as The Underground University in Seoul, South Korea, which discipled North Korean refugees. Dr. Eng informed me she was going to South Korea in just a few months and we both quickly realized our networking God had arranged this meeting of an attorney from Georgia with a psychiatrist from New York in Cuba in order to arrange for a ministry opportunity on the other side of the world. So, I put her in touch with our leadership team at Seoul USA and she greatly encouraged our students at the Underground University (most of which suffer from post-traumatic stress disorder, which results in severe anxiety—her area of specialization). Isn't that just like God? This "coincidence" helped me to see God as an amazing networker who brings people together from different background and different places in order to do his work all over the world. In retrospect, there was ministry which might not have been done had either of us chosen to stay at home, the ultimate comfort zone.

But the story does not end there. Dr. Eng was such a big hit at the Underground University that she was invited to be a speaker at our October 2013 International Christian Association Conference in Colorado Springs. In our first session, she examined the story of Gideon from the book of Judges. She explored the fear and anxiety experienced by this man, who was greeted by an angel as a "mighty man of valor" at a time when he was hiding from the Midianites (Judges 6:11-12). She then gave us seven coping skills to deal with anxiety as found in Philippians 4:6-9. You can find these in this book, also, in Chapter 4: "The Willow in Japan."

While at the conference in Colorado Springs, I mentioned to Dr. Eng that I would be in New York in a couple of months for a Board meeting of Global Youth Baseball Federation and I was bringing my wife and daughter. My daughter, Ashton, was a psychology major at the University of Georgia at the time, and she had recently felt God leading her to go to law school. At that time, she was interviewing with several top law schools and I thought it would be good for her to meet and talk to Dr. Eng. Of course Dr. Eng was most gracious and agreed to meet with us. One of the highlights of our trip to New York was that meeting with Dr. Eng, as she shared her story with my family and greatly encouraged us all. To see how she had overcome the obstacle of blindness to teach and encourage her students, and to travel all over the world to do mission work challenged us to consider, "She is blind, so what's our excuse?"

Every time I have gone on a mission trip, I have been so very blessed by the people I have met. I am so very thankful that I met Dr. Eng and saw firsthand what it means to walk by faith and not by sight. Her blind faith helps build my faith and gives so many a vision for victoriously stepping out into the unknown. God bless you Dr. Eng!

~ Stephen E. Garner, JD - Trial Lawyer
Founder, Peace Like a River Mediation Services

"Lord, have pity on me. My evil sorrows strive with my good joys; and on which side is the victory, I know not. Woe is me! Lord, have pity on me. Woe is me! lo! I hide not my wounds; Thou art the Physician, I the sick; Thou merciful, I miserable. Is not the life of man upon earth all trial? Who wishes for troubles and difficulties? Thou commandest them to be endured, not to be loved. No man loves what he endures, though he love to endure. For though he rejoices that he endures, he had rather there were nothing for him to endure. In adversity I long for prosperity; in prosperity I fear adversity. What middle place is there betwixt these two, where the life of man is not all trial?"

St. Augustine, *Confessions* (Book X, Chap. xxviii, 39)

Introduction

When Faith Shall Be Sight

Adversity sets the stage for resolve. Neither the quality nor the magnitude of the trial predicts the development of resilience nor is it guaranteed. Other factors including the emotional make-up, physical health, social support, and other intangible elements lead one to remarkable heights to scale the proverbial mountain. Nonetheless, adversity is an unapplauded contributor.

Horatio Spafford declared the paradox at the tragic death of his daughters in a shipwreck. Torn by grief yet buoyed by faith, he wrote the song "It is Well with My Soul." How can this reaction evolve from such great tragedy? It does not make sense and yet there is an invisible realm operating in human affairs that heals, restores, redeems, sans recognition. As a therapist, I am often struck by good outcomes in a patient's life that aren't expected. What is this? Mere chance? Good enough treatment? Or embedded deep faith in a metamorphic foundation?

The universe is governed by an economy endowed with paradox. Sadly, we do not appreciate this, operating mainly in a linear pattern of thinking governed by expected outcomes based on statistics, science, or our own experiences. Examples of mind-

> **The universe is governed by an economy endowed with paradox.**

stretching opposites include: the weak becoming strong, last shall be first, wisdom is foolishness, and to live one must die."

Imagine human affairs governed by such principles. Would our society collapse, our families be thrown into turmoil, our educational systems halt, and our financial infrastructure become bankrupt? It would certainly alter one's sense of identity and yet there is an undercurrent of strength and stabilization of elements of our society put into motion by these unacknowledged principles.

Here we should examine the role of adversity. We live to avoid it, resolve it legislate against it as it has no known value and poses a threat to our livelihood. We create avenues of blame for it or we maintain an attempt to objectify adversity by saying "stuff happens." Dekker in his article[1] dignifies "adversity" as a road to the development of "resilience." He advocates working with youth, not so much as to generate costly programs to "fix" them and their problems but rather to entertain a conversation with them to understand the impact, value and role of the adversity. It allows the youth to draw upon all the resources, coping skills, and ideas he owns to meet the adversity head on. The conversation also includes questioning the youth, where do you think God is in all the trouble. While there is no promise or guarantee of a good outcome, the process becomes an avenue to the promotion of resolve. Without adversity, the literature seems to say, there is no development of resilience.

The ultimate paradox is the agony of the crucifixion of Jesus followed by the victory of the resurrected Christ. No greater trial could have occurred than the sinless Son of God enduring the punishment of broken humanity in order to restore the "shalom" relationship between God and man. This willingness to embrace death in order to bestow life underscores any noble act of sacrifice which we might want to imitate.

We see it in the young man entering the military to defend his country, the missionary who risks harm in order to bless the people group in his field, the mother who sacrifices her needs for her children. God—and perhaps some of us—march into adversity for a greater good, even if sometimes that greater good cannot be named. Could we suggest that we turn away from the usual understanding of the afore-mentioned paradoxes and begin to wrap our minds around the unfamiliar, unpopular opposite?

We are told by a plethora of psychological literature regarding the normalcy of anxiety, anger, and depression when confronted with stressors. We palliate human suffering with compassionate understanding, validating the legitimacy of such emotions, creating safe havens for people to process them. If allowed some modes of counseling, strategizing solutions, coping skills, programs to ameliorate the suffering some strugglers will pass through.

While these maneuvers remain unquestionably therapeutic, none asks the individual to embrace the trial. None asks the sufferer to value the adversity as the foster parent of the prized orphan—resilience. Nor do we advocate a premature, insensitive, challenge to recover for those recently traumatized. Having said this do we embark on the daunting quest of adversity appreciation? Dekker observes, "Whatever the presuppositions may be that fuel the research on resilience, what is certain is that a growing body of research confirms that people develop resilience in their lives. Researchers are taking a closer look at the kinds of skills people learn from living through adversity rather than escaping it . . . and they are finding some interesting things."[2]

Nursing the potential of stress requires the gentle skillfulness of microvascular surgery. Is there a method to introduce the would-be toxin-turned medicant into the conversation of a sufferer? And what would it look like?

In this book, I will use autobiographical essays to describe aspects of my life as a blind physician, wife, and mother. In its original text, the essays had centered and are limited by one theme, triumph, meeting the challenge. What are decidedly absent are details of the valleys, failures, and the cavern of negative reactions to my adversity. Such avoidance, while sincere, lacks the objectivity in plumbing the depths of sadness, confusion, abandonment lumped together in the term adversity.

This valuable side of the coin is included in the narratives of others, including José, Estaban, and Oscar—Children of Honduras, Ken and Joni Tada, Dr. Dave, Dr. Alison, and Dr. S, whose personal story exemplifies the principle of resolve. Then there are so many others who have been either patients or friends, whose narratives form the basis of my perspective on this subject, even if I their names are not mentioned.

Resolve is common to all of these stories; but resolve is the mother of resilience. By faith we don't just "bounce back," but we move ahead, sometimes not knowing where the Lord is taking us.

For example, Joni Eareckson Tada, who has been a quadriplegic for more than 48 years, has become remarkably resilient through it all. Ken, her husband of 30 years, wrote to us:

> *When over five years ago doctors told Joni she had cancer, her first comment to our staff at Joni and Friends was, "Well, friends, God must be up to something big." And what*

was the big thing God did? I think he made her even more resilient, stretching the capacity of her character to not only absorb a deep disappointment, but to push through to discover how she might be enriched by it and then [the best part] pass on the encouragement to others.

After Joni's diving accident, it took her about two years to finally begin to accept her wheelchair as her own, to embrace the possibility of God doing something good out of a life with quadriplegia. But in John 16:33 Jesus said, "In this world you will have trouble. But take heart!" The wheelchair, paralysis, not to mention the depression, the chronic pain, the cancer—it's been real trouble for her. Life is not easy for my wife. But through each one of them, Joni has "learned to be content" and with the help of Jesus and friends and family who care for her, she's pressed on, developing even deeper resolve in times of trial.

Notice a couple of phrases in Ken's description: Joni has "pushed through" and "pressed on." This is determination (another word for resolve), founded in the confidence that God's will is always best. This attitude emulates the attitude of Jesus, who steadfastly "set his face" to go to Jerusalem, knowing the suffering awaiting him there. His resolve withstood all temptations, including the entreaties of his friends, especially Peter, because Jesus knew what must be done, and no force in heaven or on earth could change his mind.

When you know your calling, that's the way it is. It just is.

Questions for personal consideration and/or group discussion:

1. Carefully read the quote from St. Augustine that introduces this chapter. How do you think that his view of suffering would "fly" in today's churches?

2. The paradoxes of faith are many, and they are brought into clear focus in the teachings of Jesus. List as many of these as you can find in his teachings, and in each case explain in a sentence what that paradox might mean to you (for example: the last shall be first).

3. Define the following terms, and then describe how they relate to each other:

   Adversity

   Suffering

   Resilience

   Resolve

4. Do you believe that adversity is the only road to deeper faith?

5. Some folks seem offended when they encounter adversity. This may be more common among the young. Why do you think they respond this way? What can be done to help them see that adversity can become a positive thing, if they adopt the right perspective?

6. Ponder the quote from this chapter: "Humans march into adversity for a greater good, even if the greater good cannot be named." Can you relate to this, either personally or through the experience of someone you care about?

7. If your role is to represent Christ to those who suffer, how do you plan to do that?

Brothers and sisters, I do not consider myself yet to have taken hold of it. But one thing I do: Forgetting what is behind and straining toward what is ahead, I press on toward the goal to win the prize for which God has called me heavenward in Christ Jesus.

PHILIPPIANS 3:13-14

Chapter 1

Straining for the Goal

On the first day of the new millennium, I visited Spruce Lake Retreat Center with my church. The beautiful scenery, fresh air, and delicious meals combined with the Christian fellowship were there to restore me. Being blind from my late twenties, you might ask how a middle-aged woman can appreciate the beauty of this lovely place. With the use of my other senses I answer, "Yes, I surely can!" There is even more.

Saturday afternoon, my friend and I took a long hike with the pastor and his family. Our plan was to drop in on the nature center, followed by a walk in the great outdoors. We intended to skip the other recreational activities scheduled for that time, one of which was climbing the thirty-foot wall located in the gym. This did not seem to be a suitable activity for a blind person, although the idea did interest me. In fact, the week before the retreat, I had increased exercising my arm muscles, thinking about a possible climb. But upon arrival to the retreat, I gave up the idea.

God has never failed to awe me with his amazing plans and strength for the task, whether it is in raising my family, accomplishing professional goals, or even simple day-to-day activities.

That Saturday was no different. After returning from our walk earlier than expected, we decided to visit the charming, well-stocked Spruce Lake bookstore. As we made our purchases, my friend said, "Hey, they're still doing wall climbing!"

We entered the gym. As I sat on a chair, I remarked to another friend who was sitting next to me, "I think my son was right in telling me that I could not climb that wall without vision." My friend asked, "Elaine, would you like to go up and feel it?"

"Okay," I replied.

As I went to touch the wall, I overheard Dave, the wall climbing instructor (otherwise called a belayer) tell someone that he had actually coached a blind-folded person up the wall. In that same instant, I knew that I had to climb the three stories. To the surprise of the audience as well as myself, I signed up. What did I get myself into? I asked myself. Was this a stupid thing to do? What will I tell my family if I get injured? Or, was there a lesson to be learned from God? I did not have much time to think about this as I was soon being prepared by the instructor for the climb.

> *Brothers and sisters, I do not consider myself yet to have taken hold of it. But one thing I do: Forgetting what is behind and straining toward what is ahead, I press on toward the goal to win the prize for which God has called me heavenward in Christ Jesus* (Philippians 3:13-14).

This Scripture was the best inspiration for the climb. Although it is talking about the attitude one should have about Godly effort and perseverance in the Christian life, it emphasizes that we should strain toward that goal with all that God has given us and it is very analogous to what I experienced climbing the wall. I was determined to scale the wall and strike the bell at its apex. But as my arm and leg muscles stretched, strained, and struggled with fatigue, I found that the minutes on the wall seemed like a lifetime. The desire to quit was matched by the determination that this was a worthy goal. The godly Christian life is also a worthy goal to strain and persevere in.

Being blind, I could only feel for the crevices to grab onto and sometimes as I groped, there did not seem to be anything within reach. But by faith I believed that there must be something to grab onto and that there must be something close by. This kept my determination going. It's like having faith in darkness when it seems like there is no way to go on. With God we can count on him to provide a way even when there seems to be no way. I knew there was a peg to grab onto even when it seemed like there wasn't.

Such faith can only be maintained by focusing correctly on the right source of help. The calm, guiding voice of the instructor became my most intense focus. Blocking all other sounds and noises, I listened and trusted his voice to guide me to my goal. What transpired in those moments parallel so much of the Christian life. Straining at God's goal for us can at times be fatiguing, frightening, and seem virtually impossible. And yet, if we stay focused on his wisdom, strength, and voice, he will help us to accomplish what he desires for us. We, in turn, must block out all distractions or negative thoughts.

I must admit, there was one moment

> **If we stay focused on his wisdom, strength, and voice, he will help us to accomplish what he desires for us. We, in turn, must block out all distractions or negative thoughts.**

I panicked. I was not aware of it but I was close to the pulley, and I heard Dave's voice tensing and telling me I must not grab the pulley that was connected by a rope to my harness. I was terrified because I did not know what the pulley would feel like and how could I distinguish it from the protrusions that I was desperately grabbing onto to hold me up. Furthermore, I had mental images of knocking the rope off the pulley and possibly falling down two stories. But God provided his grace to me at that moment of panic.

Suddenly, the back of my left hand gently breezed against something that felt metallic, which was different from the wall protrusions I had been grasping. I reasoned that this was the pulley I had to avoid. After what seemed to be too many more agonizing stretches, body contortions, and gasping breaths, I heard the glorious sound of the bell as my right hand waved frantically over my head. Hallelujah! What utter joy to know that it was over and done. What relief for my aching muscles as I was lowered to the ground. There was a sense of thankfulness that knows no words or thoughts to accompany it. Rather, it is a very physical, visceral feeling that only my Maker could understand.

I will never forget this experience, which launched my new millennium. It expressed so much of what God had been doing for me in my life and what he could do for those whose earnest walk in him is challenged by disability or struggle. It described my professional work as a physician, a professor, my international ministry to do missionary counseling, and my personal life coping with blindness.

I praise God for the special lessons I have learned through my journey. He has shown me that the Bible has important teaching for both physical and emotional illnesses. When I felt the Lord leading me to write down my experiences, I asked him for the strength to do this because I had very little time in my hectic schedule. But he is so faithful and has enabled me to do this to glorify a powerful God and what he can do with a "challenged" servant. In the pages that follow, the reader will get an appreciation for how the Word of God can help Christians who are facing all sorts of obstacles or walls in their lives, and not just from my own life's narrative, but from others who have overcome significant obstacles, even learned to use these obstacles for ministry in Christ's name.

Dr. D. has been doing this for more nearly 40 years, not perfectly ... but with significant resolve. In 1978 he lost his first son, almost four years old at the time, to an undiagnosed illness. This led to a deep depression, fueled by a sense of guilt, that lasted for years. Then in 1986, having earned his doctorate in ministry in May, he faced a similar trial when his second son was taken ill toward the end of the summer, with some of the same symptoms, including evidence of brain damage. This is excerpted from his best-selling book, *If God is So Good, Why Do I Hurt So Bad?* [3]

> *Several days after my second son's CT-scan shattered my life again, I was taking a shower and reflecting on the direction our path had suddenly turned when I focused my anger on the evil one, saying something like this: "Satan, you b—, you can't have this one. Satan, you're going to be sorry."*
>
> *Not that I've had extended conversations with that pretender, nor do I make it a point to personally challenge the personification of wickedness. In fact, in Jude 9, we're told that even the archangel Michael did not bring a slanderous accusation against Satan, but said, instead, "The Lord rebuke you!"*
>
> *That is what I should have said. However, this was a turning point for me, because it helped me concentrate my anger on Satan as the tormentor rather than on God—and somehow I knew that this time the result would be different. In fact, when I first started working on this book, I was calling it, "The Christian Phoenix—Power from Pain."*
>
> *This power is not from myself, not something I produce on my own, or I will surely fail, leaving myself and those I love*

at risk in this warfare. It is not something that can be achieved—as some secular writers encourage—by steeling the will, but can only be achieved by humbly linking my helplessness with God's power, my weakness with his strength. It is another of those remarkably consistent paradoxes of faith.

What are the walls you face today? Perhaps it's dealing with grief and loss of loved ones, parenting or family issues, job problems, excessive worrying, illnesses, or other things that have become your personal wall to climb. Look to the Lord for guidance and the strength to persevere. Some people you know may need to obtain the goal of knowing Jesus, who is the loving source of divine grace, the one who will guide, the one who should be the focus and source of your resolve.

Just like my New Year's Day experience, it is God who makes it possible for us to "climb the wall" and have victory as we persevere. For as Romans 8:37 says, ". . . in all these things we are more than conquerors through him who loved us."

Questions for personal consideration and/or group discussion:

1. If you had a chance to climb a 30-foot wall, would you do so? Why? Why not?

2. For a moment, close your eyes, and imagine yourself on that wall, just a few feet up, reaching for that next hand-hold. How do you feel?

3. Now imagine yourself blindfolded, trying the same thing. How do you feel?

4. Which elements of faith would encourage you at this time?

5. If you were someone's personal counselor, and they were up 15 feet and freaking out, what might you offer?

6. How is "perseverance" related to "resolve" in this case, and what can you gain from this personally, or to offer others?

7. Consider this quote from the chapter in the context of "resolve": "Straining at God's goal for us can at times be fatiguing, frightening, and seem virtually impossible. And yet, if we stay focused on his wisdom, strength, and voice, he will help us to accomplish what he desires for us. We, in turn, must block out all distractions or negative thoughts."

   How would this kind of resolve help you (and/or others)?

You yourselves are our letter, written on our hearts, known and read by everyone. You show that you are a letter from Christ, the result of our ministry, written not with ink but with the Spirit of the living God, not on tablets of stone but on tablets of human hearts.*

2 CORINTHIANS 3:2-3

*My husband chose this as a passage that expresses his perspective on me.

Chapter 2

Hawaiian Winds

In Hawaii, "mauka" refers to the mountains, which serve as the origin of refreshingly powerful wind currents. When this weather pattern predominates, the air is dry, clean, and reminiscent of the feeling of "paradise" known to the islands. However, if the "kona" winds take over, the air is heavily saturated with humid fog emanating from the ocean, causing people to feel burdened and slowed down. Cliff and I travel to eastern Oahu often in anticipation of retiring and refocusing in a senior community in this idyllic setting. Many of our friends are confused by my insistence upon thinking about our final earthly home so early in my life. I began to make these journeys in search of a place where we will be cared for as seniors in the future, because my blindness informed me early in life that eventually by virtue of age or disability, everyone will have increased dependency on caregivers. It is better to plan for these needs than to reach that age unable to transition, lacking the ability to think clearly while in fairly good health.

In my case, it was also important to prayerfully consider my ministry and mission upon the refocusing years of my life. Geography will play an important role because I want to continue my travels to do teaching and missionary counseling in Asia and wherever the Lord directs. Hopefully my husband agrees, but even if not fully apparent to him, he enjoys the vacations we spend in Hawaii, practicing living there as opposed to treating it as a sightseeing tour.

Marriage runs very much like the alternations of the mauka and kona winds. There is refreshment and support in the relationship but also periods of adversity and weariness. Resilience in a marriage depends in part on expecting these changes as normal and weathering the difficulties, everyone in their own way. Ultimately for us, God has made it possible for us to live up to the promise "for better or for worse."

The Hawaiian mauka winds symbolize, to me, the Holy Spirit with power to restore any rift, damage, or weakness among his people and creation. It removes the aversive haze produced by the kona wind. The New Testament refers to the Holy Spirit as a wind, in Acts 2:2, "And suddenly there came a sound from heaven, as of a rushing mighty wind, and it filled the whole house where they [disciples] were sitting" (NKJV). The mighty Spirit of God, like a powerful refreshing wind, transformed the small group of believers in Jesus into the vibrant, rapidly growing church despite severe persecution and adversity.

The winds of adversity occurred early in my life and, of course, produced effects upon our marriage. Pastor Andy Kikuta, beloved chaplain of the Honolulu Police Department for 30 years, invited me to share my story to the Hawaii Kai Community Church. In front of the diverse audience of God's people—Japanese, Chinese, Hawaiian, and even a young Palestinian girl, I began my message:

In Luke 10:38-42, we meet a woman named Martha who was described as being worried and upset. She was busily running around serving Jesus and his disciples, complaining that her sister Mary was not helping. Jesus, God's son, wisely and compassionately told her the benefits of resting at his feet and listening to his teaching just like her sister Mary had been doing.

A premedical curriculum at Princeton University Medical School at the Albert Einstein College of Medicine, and an obstetrics and gynecology residency training at Bellevue and New York University hospitals began my frenzied "Martha" lifestyle. Marriage and the birth of two children, one during my last year of medical school and one during my second year of residency, blessed my life, but certainly created greater demands on my all-too-limited time. I felt the pain of divided loyalties in wanting to care for my family versus being a conscientious physician who was also loyal to her career. Medicine is a strict taskmaster, and women cannot get off the merry-go-round of professional activities easily, but God made a way for me that was totally unexpected.

In 1983, I was diagnosed as having retinitis pigmentosa, an inherited eye disease that would lead to progressive blindness. Once I heard the diagnosis, I knew it was God's way of granting my prayer to be a full-time wife and mother. God had prepared my heart to accept this news. You can imagine the surprise of my ophthalmologist when I accepted the news with God's peace. Romans 8:28 says, "And we know that in all things God works for the good of those who love him, who have been called according to his purpose."

This so-called tragedy in my life was very much for the good. I had the chance to "see" and care for my children during their precious young years; to play with them, sing songs, teach them, feed them, and do all those wonderful mothering things that many take for granted. I cherished them because I knew my life had been heading in a direction in which I could have missed it all. Now that they are grown, I can see in my mind's eye all of those great images and memories. I enjoyed motherhood so much that I would not have changed my life in any way if given the chance. My eye condition was a gift from God, affording me the privilege of time to be with my children.

When my youngest child entered school, I was ready to consider

> My eye condition was a gift from God, affording me the privilege of time to be with my children.

my professional goals again. After much thought, prayer, and advice from Dr. Ed Kong, a Christian colleague and pediatrician, I returned to training in the field of psychiatry. Ed counseled me and said that God would not have taken me through medical school for me to stop now. If psychiatry was the only field in which a blind person could do well, then it must have been God's plan. He also felt there was a great need for psychiatrists who were competent in understanding the faith of their Christian patients. Convinced of this, I applied to hospital residency training programs in psychiatry and was accepted. The transition between the fields of obstetrics and gynecology and psychiatry was quite dramatic. I had not taken even one psychology course in college and did not ever focus on psychiatry in medical school, as that was not my intended area of study. Moreover, the anxiety I now faced in training as a blind physician became daunting. Learning an entirely new body of clinical information and adjusting to the intricacies and challenges of doing it blind would be difficult to say the least.

My God was faithful to me. During my residency, objective tests showed that I had started at the bottom and, by the end of the four years, had climbed to the top in terms of psychiatric knowledge. This allowed me to practice this field for over twenty-five years, working, teaching, and writing on the integration of counseling and the Christian faith. With this experience, I also received insights on my personal life and marriage. How does a marriage sustain difficulties imposed by blindness?

Damaged Goods

Six of us sat in a restaurant in the beautiful town of Bar Harbor, Maine. We had just spent the afternoon hiking the two-mile Sand Beach trail at Acadia National Park, enjoying the sunny warm weather, salt-scented ocean air, and the incredibly beautiful vistas. My ears were regaled by nature's music played by the regular pattern of undulating waves. My husband and I, along with our dear church friends Tom, Anna, William, and Lucy, were nestled in the relaxing atmosphere on the second floor of Poor Boy's seafood restaurant as the powerful fan cooled us. We in this group make good traveling companions as we enjoy one another's fellowship, friendly humor, and fine food. In fact, these same two couples had companied us on a Mediterranean cruise to celebrate our twenty-fifth anniversary the previous year. Having warmed the banks of Rome, Kusadasi (Turkey), and the Greek locations of Santorini, Katakolon, and Piraeus, we now settled on the East Coast of the United States to feast on lobster, spinach lentil soup, broccoli vinaigrette, pasta marinara, fresh bread, and baked potatoes. Of course, some of us had a hankering for Maine's well-known blueberries. So the meal was to be topped off at the end with the restaurant's famous blueberry pie in shortbread walnut crust and vanilla ice cream. Life cannot get any better!

Because these folks were like brothers and sisters to me, I took the risk in this idyllic setting to ask a potentially troubling question, hoping not to spoil the mood but to generate a serious conversation. "Do you think that I could be considered 'damaged goods' to my husband?" I asked, hoping for their thoughtful reflections about how a spouse might view a partner who developed an unexpected disability after marriage. This was the case with me, as my eye disorder manifested itself about seven years into our marriage. Hoping that I would not spoil the evening with such a difficult question, I trusted this small group to be honest and share their comments with the understanding that I wanted to learn about their views and would not take it personally. Neither, I suspect, would my husband, who was listening with interest to questions like those below, and their responses:

- Would a handicapped person be considered damaged goods?
- Would a diagnosis such as mine cause a spouse to worry about her ability to live a normal life or raise children properly?
- Would he or she be able to handle the dependency needs of the other?
- What about self-image and how that is jeopardized by being in the companionship of someone who is not physically "whole" or perhaps no longer attractive in the usual media-defined sense?
- Would the constant stares of strangers in public slowly erode the spouse's sense of self-esteem and thus have an impact on the relationship?

Many a marriage has been threatened by illness, not to mention chronic illness. When life's storms emerge, many spouses have "jumped ship." Others have held on and weathered the torrent of emotions generated by unpredictability about the future. They have negotiated the transitions and the sense of loss, and they have made adjustments that are required. I would like to share one of the answers from our dinner table that night that serves as a valuable lesson in life. A parable of sorts, it metaphorically describes my ideal of a spouse's perspective on damaged goods.

A Dog Named Jadon

Jadon is a young golden retriever, given to my friend's son. It did not take long for this boisterous, affectionate, young puppy to win the heart of my friend, Anna, who referred to him as "our grandchild." Despite his annoying habit of chewing on furniture and shoes and his sometimes disobedient behavior, he was lovable in so many respects. Daily he anticipated seeing Anna when she returned from work; his ears would perk up and he would dash to her, immediately giving her licks of love. In the morning he would bark his plea for her to feed him then take him for a walk. She would respond often times as early as 3:00 a.m. Jadon received so much love and attention from his "grandmother," many a grandchild (even the non-hairy variety) would do well to have even a small portion of this loving attention. There was always a treat for Jadon, whether from the local Petland or even Maine's Bar Harbor. After Jadon was traumatized when a smoke alarm was set off by cooking, he would have the canine equivalent of a panic attack whenever dinner was being cooked. As a result, Anna grilled food upstairs and ordered a lot of take-out in order to keep Jadon calm. This was one truly loved dog.

One day, Anna took Jadon to the veterinarian for his vaccinations. To her surprise, the vet asked, "Did you know your dog is missing a testicle?" Stunned, she answered, "No. The pet store said the puppy was in perfect condition." She wondered what missing a testicle meant. She did not understand what the other might be doing in the abdomen, as the vet had suggested, or why it was missing. Then she became angry: How could the pet store have sold a dog that was advertised as perfect with such an obvious defect? She felt she had received damaged goods. Then she looked at Jadon and she immediately realized, I love him. No matter what, I do love him, even if he is not perfect. The moral of this parable is: Valued merchandise dissolves the wrath of a cheated consumer. Just like Jadon, I am not damaged goods, at least not to the one who loves me.

My husband has chosen two biblical passages that best express his perspective of me. The first is 2 Corinthians 3:2-3:

> *You yourselves are our letter, written on our hearts, known and read by everyone. You show that you are a letter from Christ, the result of our ministry, written not with ink but with the Spirit of the living God, not on tablets of stone but on tablets of human hearts.*

He says that I am like a letter written by God for everybody to read, that my life is a testimony to him and those around us, and that my blindness serves as a vehicle to provide an encouraging message from God regarding overcoming challenges. I am not a letter written in ink but one written by the Holy Spirit and impressed upon the hearts of people.

He also chose Hebrews 12:1-3:

> *Therefore, since we are surrounded by such a great cloud of witnesses, let us throw off everything that hinders and the sin that so easily entangles. And let us run with perseverance the race marked out for us, fixing our eyes on Jesus, the pioneer and perfecter of faith. For the joy set before him he endured the cross, scorning its shame, and sat down at the right hand of the throne of God. Consider him who endured such opposition from sinners, so that you will not grow weary and lose heart.*

This indicates that of my life God is the author of the faith he sees in me, a faith which he also possesses and holds dear. Given this perspective, I have never felt like damaged goods in the presence of my husband, or for that matter, in the company of those who love me.

Back to our dinner at Bar Harbor, when I first posed the question about a person being damaged goods, several minutes of discussion and feedback about my blindness followed. Finally, Tom interrupted with the quip, "OK, we've talked enough about Elaine. Let's get to the point of answering her question about how we feel about damaged goods. Let's talk about Cliff!" We roared with laughter, as this comment was so illustrative of the humor and fun that is essential in coping with disability.

My husband and I had many funny moments as I started to lose my eyesight. I continue to do most of the cooking, laundry, and some housecleaning. In fact, I enjoy cooking very much and have found many ways to do it by choosing recipes that I label as "forgiving" because they can tolerate much error and still taste delicious. I continue to do the chores because I value the sense of independence it gives me. And because repetition makes it easier for blind persons to retain the ability to do a task, I cherish doing simple tasks of day-to-day living. However, we have had a few mishaps.

Watercress is a beautiful green vegetable that makes a delicious soup when it is cooked in a pork broth. Its green color is very similar to the green scrubbing sponges we keep on our sink to wash pots and pans. Because they offer no contrast in color to the watercress, the sponges wound up in the soup one time. As my husband lifted up the surprise ingredient, he recoiled in horror, and this has been the subject of many lively evenings recounting to our friends how his blind wife nearly killed him.

Then there was the time when I was removing nail polish with an acetone cotton ball. I could not find the garbage can, so I dropped it in what I thought was an empty cup. Instead, it was my husband's Coke. When he went to take the next sip, a strange, chemical odor wafted into his nose and, unfortunately, into his mouth. "Uh-oh," I said. "Well a little acetone won't hurt you."

He also reminds me about the time I used a bath towel to wipe around the kitty litter box and then hung it up instead of discarding it. When he used it to dry his face he detected a peculiar smell and approached me suspiciously.

Despite these assaults, my husband reacts with good humor to these blindness-related incidents, and we both enjoy a good laugh as we entertain our friends with our stories. He wears the black tie-dyed socks and the pink underwear that I inadvertently bleached, thinking I had a full load of whites. He does not seem to mind when his co-workers ask about the interesting patterns on his socks. My children have been a little less tolerant, when they have pulled their ruined outfits out of the laundry basket. I guess that is what made them learn to do their own laundry. After tolerating all these mishaps so well, I have to conclude that I am not damaged goods to my own husband.

During our Maine trip, the men were talking a great deal about cars because my husband wanted to buy a new one for our family. A lot of the discussion focused on "Consumer Reports" and which car had the best rating for performance, looks, reliability, and so on. The men enjoyed discussing which the best model was, Tom and William pointing them out to Cliff as we drove around. Our friends kept insisting that the best cars were the Honda Accord, Toyota Avalon, or Nissan Maxima. Again and again they extolled the virtues of these models, and they pretty much had me convinced. My husband, who until this time was barely agreeable to buying a new car, rather than choosing a used one, which was his preference, kept saying he really did not want the popular models. He said he would prefer a Saturn.

Our friends wanted to know why, as they believed that the Saturn did not compare with the models everyone else was buying. He said, "I am not like everyone else. In fact, I prefer to choose the different car because it has a different image that better suits me. I like the Saturn because it's different, as I am different . . . as long as it is reliable!" As his wife, I am like the Saturn—different, not the most popular in the market, but truly reliable in Cliff's eyes. I am a letter of Christ's love, written by God and ordained for my husband.

This reminds me of the hundreds of love letters we exchanged during the years I was away at college and we were dating long distance. Because of our multiple moves and the many years that have intervened, I have unfortunately lost them. It's not so much a tragedy as possibly a mixed blessing, because I would be frustrated by not being able to read them. I certainly would not feel comfortable in having them read to me. So it is better for me to have the memory of them. Besides, the real love letter is written on hearts and not paper or even tablets of stone. In many ways, God has given me a very suitable life partner. A social worker by profession, he is gratified by helping. When we first got married, I never thought I would become the object of his social work. I also understand him well. My training in psychiatry has helped me to understand his psychological makeup, i.e., why he prefers to be different. Because I understand it, I do not react with disbelief or disdain or take his idiosyncrasies personally. We are a match slightly damaged perhaps but made in heaven.

The Mop Story

Preparing to give a series of talks to an Ambassadors for Christ (AFC) singles conference, I was slightly perturbed by the fact that I was middle-aged and somehow too old to appeal to young singles. What did I have in common with them? What could I tell them about womanhood or how to date and find a mate? It had been more than twenty-five years since I went through that process. Moreover, could they relate to me not just because of the stage in life difference, but also in the way I dressed or even the way I looked? My visual handicap could be a barrier and an obstacle in my ability to relate to most people, but especially young people who may not have had much experience dealing with the handicapped. They might, therefore, feel awkward. God came through again and allayed my worries. I planned three talks—one on managing anxiety, one on womanhood and the Proverbs woman, and one on my personal testimony in Christ.

It was after my final talk that a young man wanted to know about my husband. At first I thought he wanted me to address my husband's perspective on being married to a blind person. The young man clarified and said what he really wanted to know was how I met my husband and what attracted me to him. So I recounted the story. When I first became a Christian as a teenager, I attended True Light Lutheran Church. After some time of getting to know everybody, the folks in the church began to talk excitedly about a Clifford Eng, who was coming back from military duty. I kept wondering, Who is this Clifford Eng who seemed to be friends with all the young people in the church? One day, I walked into the sanctuary and discovered the answer. There was Clifford Eng mopping the chapel floor. As soon as I saw him, I said to myself, "That's the man for me. He mops and cleans!" After that story, the audience applauded loudly and laughed heartily. The next night at the formal awards dinner, a new award was created for the most godly male single: a brand new mop! During skit night, young men dressed in tuxedos paraded across the stage between acts pushing mops, as if in a cleaning frenzy, to the amusement of the audience.

I hear that my mop story has become part of Ambassadors for Christ singles history.

Questions for personal consideration and/or group discussion:

1. How do you relate do the author's early consideration of "retirement" needs and opportunities?

   ___ It's prudent.

   ___ It's not aligned with believing the Lord will take care of her.

   ___ Hawaii sounds great to me!

   ___ If she can manage her world-wide ministries from there as well as elsewhere, great!

   ___ Other:

2. How likely do you think it is, on a scale of 1-100, for disabled people to consider themselves "damaged goods." Mark your answer on this line:

   |----------------------------50----------------------------|

   Was it not interesting that the author, with all her accomplishments, might still consider herself to be "damaged goods." How does knowing this affect your own self-view, and/or how does it help you better understand some of the feelings of your disabled friends?

3. The author describes "funny moments" with her husband as she was losing her eyesight? Does anything about this hit you, emotionally?

4. Describe what "The Mop Story" means to you, and how you might use this type of example in helping others.

*We are hard-pressed on every side,
yet not crushed; perplexed, but not
in despair; persecuted, but not
abandoned; struck down,
but not destroyed.*

2 Corinthians 4:8

Chapter 3

Mind the Gap

On the Piccadilly train line running from Heathrow Airport to central London, my son and I were greeted by the conductor's voice at each stop: "Mind the gap, everyone; mind the gap." Slightly befuddled by the sleep deprivation from our overnight flight from New York to London, we listened with consternation. We were heading for Kenya on a later evening flight and had decided to spend the day in the city, and we were confused by the announcement.

What gap are they referring to? Is he asking us to be mindful of such a gap or do we mind that the gap exists?

The answer is obvious after one realizes that there is a significant separation between train and platform at each station, and the phrase warns passengers to be careful on exiting the train, so as not to get hurt if they put a foot (or a white cane) into the gap.

The double meaning for me describes the periodic doubts I have had about raising my children as a blind mother. Is the now well-adjusted, sleepy young man sitting next to me on the train because he chose to accompany me on this missionary care trip to Kenya, never mind the gap caused by his mother's limitations?

Is the same young man mindful that his mother cannot do all that other sighted people can do? The same question goes for my daughter, but I will devote the first part of this chapter to my son's reactions. You might ask him, but let me free-associate and develop my thoughts on the subject first. So . . . back to our London excursion.

Our train finally arrived at Piccadilly Circus, which is central to many of London's tourist attractions: Big Ben, Buckingham Palace, Westminster Abbey, St. James's Park, and so on. Camera in hand, Brian escorted me from location to location and I, although not seeing, vicariously enjoyed the fact that he was seeing them for the first time in his life. What surprised me was that he did not seem as excited as I was, and I wondered why. Perhaps he was tired since he had not slept on the flight. Perhaps he was not very interested in London, though he had said he wanted to go.

Perhaps it was not a young man's idea of fun to be with his mother on a vacation, albeit only a brief one, before going on to mission service. Or could that worry that has haunted my mind over the years, and more intensely during my children's adolescence, be the case? Are my children ashamed to be seen with a handicapped mother?

I know the looks that I get from strangers because many of my friends, colleagues, and family members have described them to me: looks of pity, sorrow, and discomfort. I have always been interested in a full description of others' reactions to me, as human thinking and behavior is my area of study. It is actually quite interesting and fun to observe because it is intellectually stimulating even if not personally experienced. I start to question the opinions of my disability in those relationships that are important to me or when it involves people whose reactions to my blindness may negatively impact my life in some way, whether in job discrimination or unanticipated rejection. There are times when my doubts are due to my own projection of my thoughts about my handicap onto others.

So, are my kids ashamed to be with me at times? To speculate, it probably has happened. It is an honest and human reaction under certain circumstances and in certain stages of development. A teacher once told me that it was lucky I became blind when my children were young, because it is harder when it occurs during their adolescence. I tend to agree with this, as teenagers are quite concerned about self-image and any imperfection may be exaggerated in their minds, including a defect in their parent. Parents of teens are often seen as defective even if they are not so. It is not easy even for the sighted ones.

What happens, then, when the parent has a disability? I can speak only for myself. I suppose I could have had my feelings hurt by this extra reason for rejection, but instead it actually prepared me for their adolescence. I had been girded already by the notion that, although I had a handicap, my identity was not dominated by such an imperfection. I reminded myself that I could not do certain things because I was blind. However, if someone leveled the playing field, I could perhaps do those things through adaptive technology or even with the benefit of having a sighted companion to perform those steps that required sight, and I would follow with them.

My life is a challenge because of the handicap, but I am not a person challenged by life. Having thought this way for many years does gird those moments of doubt when I worry that loved ones do the same. Brian and I stopped at many of the major sites of London. By noon, we had worked up an appetite. We were in the mood for Chinese food, possibly a longing for home after many hours of travel, so we started walking in the direction of London's Chinatown. As was the case with the Israelites, we began a wilderness wandering looking for the promised land of a good restaurant, but we kept going in circles. "Why don't we ask someone?" I asked Brian. "We don't have to," replied my son, "We'll find it."

How could he be so sure? When alone, I am used to asking people quite readily in the beginning since, given my limited sight, I have no hope of reaching an elusive target. Why waste time? It is not so for sighted people maybe even less so for men and definitely not so for my son, who continued to lead the way to I-am-not-sure-where. Although I recognized our differences in perspective, it was still hard to be respectful when famished . . . but we continued on.

I wonder how the differences in my perspective have affected my children and whether I have done a good job in conveying that what I do is merely the perspective of a blind person making unique adjustments, but that my perspective or behavior does not need to be their perspective or behavior. I think of the times when I had to hold the hands of my school-age children just to know that they were safe with me, while other mothers could keep a distant eye on children and allow them freedom to play. Would I create neurotic children this way? I certainly generated unhappy ones at times when they made me aware that other kids were not holding onto their mothers' hands. I guess I must have relinquished my grip in due time. After all, it is unfathomable to envision holding onto an adult man or woman's hands for his or her safety.

It is amusing to me that although most teens are overly concerned about their friends' evaluations of them, my own children's friends seem to be the greatest supporters of my ability to function. In fact, many of them insist to my own kids that I must be able to see, because I function so well. I guess the consolation prize in having teenagers is the respect of their friends. During those years, the parental grass is always greener on the other side unless that other side has committed a heinous offense. Happily, the teen years were fairly painless and relatively short, and our children grew up to be the kind of adults we of prayed for and dreamed about.

Brian's college years were very productive. He received a degree in computer science and carried two minors, all in three and one-half years. Beyond that, his college experience taught him leadership in Christian work as he served as a worship leader and president of the Asian-American Christian Fellowship, a campus ministry of InterVarsity Christian Fellowship. One day, he asked if I could speak to this group, at their request, about my experience in publishing *"Martha, Martha": How Christians Worry*. I was shocked, because for years I'd had the impression that I was incapable of offering to this young man or his peers any possible shred of wisdom. Now they were inviting me to speak.

Was he as uncomfortable about this as I was? Was his arm being twisted by his fellow students? Then the doubts flowed. What could I say that would impact the audience and improve my image in my son's eyes? Should I be funny? Serious? Intellectual? Motherly? No, not the latter—that role might be too embarrassing. What was I going to do? Prayer, that's the ticket. At that point I needed nothing less than divine intervention, and that's what I received.

I walked into their storefront meeting place and was greeted by a group of college students, some quite friendly and others shy and retiring. Without sight, only the former are recognized easily. The others are lost to perception unless they pipe up later. The leaders gathered together to pray for me and for the night. Then God worked his magic. By the time it was done, the students were really engaged, entertained, and encouraged. I had a lot of fun, and my books were selling like review manuals at finals time. Brian told me he thought it went really well, which was the best reward I could have had. The Lord had used him to be my agent in the college world, and it was a success. I should have known that it was not the risky business I feared it would be, but that is where my faith will have to grow.

Red shoes and the "Blind Neurotic Thing"

My son's reply to the query, "What is it like having a blind mother?" was somewhat different from my speculations. Most of his complaints of me as a mother are the usual things that mothers do: I always think I am right; I treat him like a child. Regarding the blindness, he says that because he has been living with my blindness since he could remember, he does not feel he has missed anything due to my limitations. He seems to think that I carry on pretty much as any mother would. However, he does have complaints because of my blindness, which both children will heartily articulate: my choice of clothes and how I match, or rather do not match, them. Their biggest source of horror is my pair of red shoes, or more specifically, a pair of bright red Reebok high-top sneakers I inherited from a friend. I have put on this most comfortable pair of footwear with, I guess, the most outlandish combinations of clothing, including my green down coat, a tank top with a tropical medley of orange and blue flowers, and pink sweatpants. To me, if the clothes feel good, they ought to look good, but the rational side of my mind tells me and, more important, my children tell me that this is not so! My daughter insisted that she pick out my outfit for her high school graduation. I gladly assented, as I certainly wanted to make her day as smooth and pleasant as possible. Besides, I hate shopping and choosing my clothing. The only garments that appeal to my blunted vision are usually in the gold and black combinations which wind up as fabric usually meant for an upholstered couch and not women's wear. The only relatively safe colors I can buy are all-black or all-white items, which require no effort to match to other items as they will almost always "go." It is funny, because I do defer to my family in choosing my clothing, and especially to my daughter.

So there was a time when Gen was about five to eight years old when I wore a lot of pink frills. Then I went through a black phase during her adolescence. Happily, she is an adult now and it will not be long before I will dress appropriately for my age. I thank God for classic business suits as they keep me from utter ridicule during office hours or when speaking in front of people!

They have another complaint of their blind mother that all three of us call the "blind neurotic thing." Its origins are probably that

I am somewhat neurotic to begin with; they say you have to be in order to become a physician. This is accentuated by the addition of a handicap. For example, I insist on having things done my way because I think that I am correct even when I am not. A recent conversation about purchasing a new family car that is safe and sturdy led me to insist to my kids that Volkswagen Beetles are not safe. To my recollection, these "bugs" look like a can of peanuts waiting to be opened by the slightest impact. Of course, I have not seen a VW in twenty years and was told that they no longer look like my mental picture of a VW. What irks my children is that I can be so emphatic based on old (to them) facts. I have to say in my defense that my image of them feels very current. My picture of the present is composed of images I saw decades ago. The positive side of this is that, to my mind, neither my husband nor I have aged. What a blessing, as I do not fret over our looks as many of our middle-age peers do.

Back to my children and this "blind neurotic thing": the car conversation does not compare with the genuinely upset feelings generated by the following anecdote. My son's church basketball team was in a heated, neck-and-neck competition in a summer tournament. They were counting on winning the next game to place first, and Brian was one of their key players. However, earlier that month I had received a frightening phone call that Brian had been cut in the eye during basketball and would have to be taken to the hospital. My husband and I hurried to the emergency room with thoughts too unimaginable to articulate. Fortunately, Brian's laceration was just above his eye and not to the eye itself. It was sutured by a plastic surgeon. Brian was admonished by the doctor not to play ball or do anything that might reopen the wound in his eye area. Now, a month later, his friends were pleading with him to help win the game. Although torn by their dilemma, I insisted that he could not play based on his doctor's recommendation and my fear of having him hurt the wound again. Needless to say, he was quite upset that I did not even consider his assessment of being well enough to play. His friends pleaded with me to let him play, but I held my ground with an unusual determination, which was quite uncharacteristic of me.

It was not until after a year of enduring his lingering hostility about this event that we discussed it, and I then realized that part of my unrelenting stance was because the injury had something to do with his eye. My irrational fear was that he might have been blinded. I had the intuitive feeling that I was quite traumatized at the time of his injury but assumed it was a usual maternal reaction. Only my composed doctorly self helped me to stick to the facts during his treatment in the emergency room. In discussing it with Brian, I recognized that as much as I thought I had adjusted to blindness, I could not bear the thought of it afflicting my children. So this is what we call the "blind neurotic thing," and I hope to be able to recognize this in myself in the future. It might help me let go in those instances that I should. Thankfully, retinitis pigmentosa has the kind of recessive inheritance pattern in which it should not affect my children unless my husband also carried the gene.

This revelation also reminded me of when my daughter was in second grade and she said she had trouble reading because her vision was blurred. Rather than taking her to the regular optometrist, I proceeded directly to the top pediatric neuropthalmologist in the area—talk about overkill! Somehow I needed to be reassured that her sight was not affected as mine was. So when I got the news that children often get blurry vision when tired, I was relieved. All that she needed was temporary reading glasses from the drugstore if she had the symptoms again. Later she confessed to me that the only reason she complained of blurred vision was that she wanted glasses like her friends had. It serves her right that we bought the cheapest, ugliest pair available at that drugstore. This is the same child who told me she had taken her erythromycin for her strep throat even though I found the big pink pill in the kitchen garbage can. I guess they think they can pull fast ones on their blind mother, but a mother's intuition and knowledge of her children can make up for a lot of visual deficits!

Memories and Fantasies

"Your mother is a CIA agent," my daughter's college friend Nick told her. "She functions too well to be really blind. I'll bet all that traveling she does to give talks is really undercover missions she does, posing as a blind person!" Nick and I met only briefly, when he spent part of his summer vacation with our family. How he came up with this idea probably had very little to do with our meeting but had a lot to do with my daughter's accounts of my work to her friends. She is pretty clear in stating that, "My blind mother can do more than many that are sighted."

Although I cherish the fact that she seems proud of me, I suspect she must embellish the story a bit. In any case, God deserves the credit, lest I develop a swelled head. With her stories about her mom, Genevieve cannot convince new friends that her mother is blind. Even in high school, one of her best friends, Peter, insisted that I was not at all blind but was into the charade for the blue handicap sticker that allows us to park our car in privileged spots. He spoke of our family as picture perfect, living in a house with the proverbial white picket fence. Although humorous to me, who cannot even see my beige, fenceless, Tudor home, I appreciate the image conveyed. Where else but in the mind of an imaginative Korean teenager could we get an all-American snapshot of the perfect family that includes a married couple with one son and one daughter, where the mother is posed in her dark glasses and white cane? All-American family indeed!

Let me share my memories about first getting the cane. For years after my diagnosis was made, I hesitated to obtain a cane. It was partly because I did not think I needed it, since not all of my vision had deteriorated, and partly because getting a cane would call attention to my handicap. Using the cane would give me an instant new identity to others and highlight to myself that I was a blind person who needed to adjust to others' reactions to me, including the reactions of strangers. I was not ready for it until one day, when crossing the street, I almost got hit by a bus because I did not see it. The driver probably figured I saw him and therefore should have moved more quickly, like most New Yorkers would have done.

Little did he know that I was not like most New Yorkers, nor did I give him any clue or warning to slow down. A mobility trainer taught me how to use the cane to feel and make a clear path for myself as I walked. There is a rhythm to the sweeping motion, back and forth, that is matched by the cadence of one's gait. Everything is precise in order to ensure safety, automaticity, and consistency in its use. Any veering from the rules in which I was trained often led to accidents. Before long, the pain of such injuries reminded me never to slack off in its proper use. It truly opened up my world, as I found I could travel farther on my own when walking in my neighborhood.

Shortly after mastering the cane, I started my residency training in psychiatry. My fellow residents laughed with me as we found that in the hospital, getting to the cafeteria for lunch would be much faster if they put me in front to clear the path through the crowds with my sweeping cane. I think a good sense of humor helps to dissipate any discomfort among others.

Once, I met with a senior resident for the first time to get adjusted to being on call in the hospital. Somehow, my cane picked up something from the floor that stuck to it and it dragged along down the halls as we walked. When I realized what happened, I remarked that this special cane had the dual purpose to not only guide me but also to pick up garbage at the same time. Corny as the joke was, he laughed loudly, partly because of the humor but mostly at the relief that I can joke about my dependency on it.

Most fascinating was the reaction of my church friends. Although three years earlier we had told them about my diagnosis and the prognosis of eventual blindness, they did not fully react until the day they saw me for the first time walking up to the altar for communion with my white cane. My husband got many remarks and questions that day. They all asked something to the effect of, "She really isn't that blind, is she?" I guess there comes a time when psychological denial no longer works, and nothing helps to overcome it like the traditional white cane.

Children have a fascination for the cane. I often hear the young voices in the bank or supermarket asking their mothers in loud unabashed voices, "Mommy, what's that stick for?" Sometimes their mothers explain its purpose in matter-of-fact detail, but many try to hush their children and move them to a distant place before venturing an explanation, as if they might hurt my feelings if they explained it within my earshot. Young children relate to handicapped persons quite well until they are taught to be uncomfortable. I have been entertained by young ones whom I have befriended that ask if they can borrow my cane to help them walk. It is as funny as the many times my young daughter would find a wooden stick and use it just as I used my cane when she walked with me. It is very funny for others to see a tiny girl with big sunglasses holding a small tree branch and swinging it from side to side. Of course, she stopped this behavior as a teenager. Later, this childlike identification was taken over by my young niece, who proudly walks with my cane.

Lessons in Faith

What can I, as a mother, teach my children through my experience with the challenges of blindness? I am in some ways a shepherd to my family—a teacher, a role model, as well as a mother. As with any group I mentor, encourage, or inspire, I do not want only to entertain them with stories about my life but hope to instill lessons applicable to their own lives. Here are the lessons in faith I have learned:

<u>Keep Putting One Foot Before the Other</u>
How does that little girl with the oversized sunglasses and the wooden cane that she does not really need, walk? For that matter, how does her blind mother with the real white cane get from one place to another? By putting one foot in front of the other and repeating the process: left foot, right foot, left foot, right foot. Although this seems trite, it is not at all simple. There are many things involved. But the key is faith, and more explicitly, trust. One must have a lot of trust to walk. First, you must trust the cane to tell you that the path in front of you is indeed clear. Then you must trust that the direction that you are heading in is the correct one, or you will be wasting time and probably get lost. Worrying about this will cause you to hesitate to go forward. You may also have to trust the person or persons who come to your assistance at any point in your travels.

Many times you need to make decisions as to whether you can trust any of these things, and you could, at any point, doubt the trustworthiness of them. Trust requires thinking and assessment;

an educated sense of human nature; teachability so that you can learn from your mistakes; and an ability to remember all those things and people on whom you can rely. Yet all this is not enough. At any point along the road, you can be paralyzed. Disorientation from untrustworthy cues, a loss of faith in the cane when you have tripped over a crevice it missed, or a lack of a person to assist you when you are at some confusing crossroad all can halt any progress you have made.

What, then, is required to ensure progress, whether in traveling or in life? My only answer and what has worked for me is absolute faith in God; I trust him and believe he is supervising my entire adventure. The knowledge that he sees what is going on, even though I do not, is enough to reassure me that I can put my left foot in front of my right foot and go on. Sometimes in a moment of nagging fear, I recall the hymn, "Guide Me, Oh Thou Great Jehovah" and walk to the rhythm of the melody. Soon all fear and doubt are diminished by the tones of the song and the message it conveys. Or I think about the angels that God employs to protect his children and I am reminded that, "There are angels all around" me, a line from another song. Somehow the content of these two thoughts work to remind me that I am safe in my travels with a sovereign God watching over me and allowing me to make progress from point A to point B. I mean this both literally as I walk about and figuratively as I negotiate my personal and professional life. As the verse says, "We walk by faith . . ." The Bible continues with "not by sight."

Then, how is a blind person to "see"? Heavenly vision is my definition of what faith allows me to see. It takes on many forms, but clearly its source is the Lord. How many times have I lost something and have asked God to put me right in front of that item, since I have no other way of locating it when alone? Within a short time, the object would be in my hands, to my surprise, at least initially. Now with repeated occurrences, I am no longer surprised, but am still very thankful. Trying to teach this spiritual concept to a sighted person looking for something is like teaching a gourmet chef how to open a can. It is preposterously simple and often deemed by the individual to be unnecessary, but strand him or her on a desert island with only wood for kindling, a can opener, and some canned goods, and he or she will take on a different vision. My eye condition puts me in a similar position, and I have discovered the perspective that a simple trust in God is vital no matter how much one thinks one owns or possesses! Heavenly vision also refers to those cues I get that help to gain insight into a situation or a person that others obtain from their eyesight. Some people cannot even identify certain insights despite their eyesight, or perhaps their vision may mislead them. Call these heavenly insights "intuition," but I believe they can be broken down into the following components. I refer to cues from our surroundings that do not require vision:

Sound
It is amazing how much one can tell about a person's mood by listening to the tone and tension in his or her voice, as well as by paying careful attention to what is being said. It really does not take a rocket scientist to know how a person is doing by carefully listening. Yet in our visually dependent, overstimulated, and rushed lives, we do not take the time to develop our listening skills.

Scent
Scent is still another cue. Favorite perfumes, soaps, or deodorants have often helped me identify a person as he or she walks into a room. Odors and the lack of such perfumes can tell me whether a person is ill, depressed, or too busy to take care of himself or herself. All of these can be addressed as I serve my family, my friends, or my patients. Many have asked me if my other senses became sharper when I became blind. The answer is yes and no. I do not believe they got sharper, but I have gotten much better at using them since I have to rely on them more often. For exam-

ple, I can always rely on my sense of touch to pick the best fruits and vegetables in a grocery store. Add to this the smell of ripeness and it is a cinch to obtain perfect produce.

<u>Wisdom</u>
Heavenly vision also has a lot to do with wisdom, and by this I mean the wisdom and truth that are found in the Bible. You get so many versions of the truth as you listen to others describe it to you from their perspective. Therefore, I need an anchor, and for me the time-honored, well-used, blessed Word of God becomes my choice when I need to "see the light." It is such a great source of heavenly insight, and my ability to trust in it has fueled the way for many of the accomplishments of my life. Without it, I would be fearful even to proceed.

One of our friends, Dr. Alison, lost her practice and her dreams for a family, due to a chronic illness. This is her 20-year perspective on the whole experience:

> *"We are hard-pressed on every side, yet not crushed; perplexed, but not in despair; persecuted, but not abandoned; struck down, but not destroyed"* (2 Corinthians 4:8).

I have a chronic illness.

Twenty years ago, I was working as a Family Physician in a busy clinic. My husband and I were looking forward to starting our family. My life came to a crashing halt when I developed encephalitis. My brain was damaged by a microscopic virus, which left me with a seizure disorder, severe migraine headaches, and other significant life-long challenges. When I was no longer able to work, due to my illness, I plummeted into a pit of deep despair. I slowly got back on my feet again through the loving support of my husband and my growing faith and dependence of my Lord and Savior. Now, I take one day at a time, trusting in the Lord to set the agenda for my life.

I am in my early 50s, and have been struggling this past year with "change-of-life" symptoms. Hot flashes, dry skin, insomnia, and emotional liability have been added to the thorns I battle on a daily basis. What bothers me most about these symptoms is that they represent the beginning of the end of my reproductive capabilities. Intellectually, I understand this, but emotionally, tears come to my eyes at the thought that the doors of biological motherhood are now closed to me. My chronic illness prevented me from having children. My heart aches in pain.

Last week in church I heard a beautiful hymn, the words of which brought peace to my soul. "Day by Day and With Each Passing Moment" was penned by Karolina Berg after her painful experience of watching her father fall off a boat and drown:

> Day by day, and with each passing moment,
> Strength I find to meet my trials here;
> Trusting in my Father's wise bestowment,
> I've no cause for worry or for fear.
> He, whose heart is kind beyond all measure,
> Gives unto each day what He deems best,
> Lovingly, its part of pain and pleasure,
> Mingling toil with peace and rest.
>
> Ev'ry day the Lord Himself is near me,
> With a special mercy for each hour;
> All my cares He fain would bear and cheer me,
> He whose name is Counselor and Pow'r.
> The protection of His child and treasure
> Is a charge that on Himself He laid;
> "As thy days they strength shall be in measure,"
> This the pledge to me He made.

Help me then, in every tribulation,
So to trust Thy promises, O Lord,
That I lose not faith's sweet consolation,
Offered me within Thy holy Word.
Help me, Lord, when toil and trouble meeting,
E'er to take, as from a father's hand,
One by one, the days, the moments fleeting,
Till I reach the promised land.[4]

I am thankful for my chronic illness. My body is weak but my faith in Christ is gaining power by the day. My resilience is fragile, but my determination to do his will remains strong. I take one day at a time, trusting in the grace of my Lord and Savior to help me through each day. ONE DAY AT A TIME.

God's Insight

Finally, heavenly vision does include an indefinable aspect, what I could only describe as God's provision of insight from his resources, other than those I have just described. When all the known tangibles are factored out, there remains a large category of things you see because God has put the conviction and vision in your spirit. When this happens, I trust this as if it were sight. It is then confirmed by many circumstances. When I reach my destination or goal, there is great rejoicing in my heart that his vision is not only trustworthy but also realizable!

The third faith lesson I want to pass onto my children from my experiences is that we must live by faith. Psalm 127:1 says, "Unless the Lord builds the house, its builders labor in vain. Unless the Lord watches over the city, the watchmen stand guard in vain."

This verse teaches that faith in God must be the foundation of a person's marriage, family, vocation, ministry, and security. I have been blessed by his presence and orchestration of all these aspects of my life. Do not get me wrong; I am not perfect in all these areas, since at times I try to take control over one or all of these spheres of life, despite my knowledge and determination to let God rule. Yet my determination to have him be the foundation for my personal and professional life has always been my deepest desire, and God has honored this resolve with his grace and help. My marriage, family, vocation, and ministry have given me deep satisfaction and joy, so much so that I have no regrets in any of these.

What about security? Can I stand safe and secure in all these things I have listed? Psalm 127 tells us that the sighted watchmen stand in vain to guard the city if the Lord is not watching over it. This answers the question. The blind person whose foundation is God has infinitely more security than the sighted who does not share this foundation, knowing that the Lord is watching over his or her domain. I have full trust in this fact and therefore remain secure. This security is a priceless treasure, and I believe it is what prompts me to keep persevering with joy in the Christian life. God has taught me such valuable lessons in faith in my disability. Truly he is able to help overcome any challenge in life. May my children be blessed with this legacy, and may I continue to model it as I shepherd them along.

Questions for personal consideration and/or group discussion:

1. Suppose you are the author's companion as she visits London (or any other major city), and you notice how people seem to look at her: pity, sadness, discomfort, whatever.

How do you feel? What do you say or do in order to raise their level or respect for her?

2. If the author has questions about how even her family might be viewing her, how can you help in relation to other parents or families who might face this issue?

3. Consider this quote from the chapter: "My life is a challenge because of the handicap, but I am not a person challenged by life."

    What do you think she means by this statement, and also, if you can identify, what does it mean to you?

Do not be anxious about anything, but in everything, by prayer and petition, with thanksgiving, present your requests to God. And the peace of God, which transcends all understanding, will guard your hearts and your minds in Christ Jesus. Finally, brothers, whatever is true, whatever is noble, whatever is right, whatever is pure, whatever is lovely, whatever is admirable if anything is excellent or praiseworthy think about such things. Whatever you have learned or received or heard from me, or seen in me put it in practice. And the God of peace will be with you.

Philippians 4:6-9

Chapter 4

The Willow in Japan

Tokyo is a bustling city, a mixture of modernity and ancient traditions. Efficiency in planning and design are observed in all aspects of life here. Space is at a premium, so the apartments, garages, packaged consumer goods, and roads and footpaths are designed to be just big enough to carry out their purpose, but to the American, the sense of space seems miniaturized. In this urban—even Western, if you will—metropolis, one cannot help but notice the time-honored oriental demeanor of the Japanese men, women, and children who march quickly with a mission.

Yet they are deferential, respectful to all, especially the aged and frail. They are serenely silent even in the subways. The subways in Tokyo are amazingly immaculate, constantly being washed by scores of workers, and so timely that you can set your watch by the arrival of the trains at each station. The air in summer is forever moving with strong aquatic breezes, mixed with heat and humidity. Yet for a city, the air is not offensively polluted, again a tribute to the Japanese penchant for cleanliness. This is true for most locations, unless one walks into the fog of cigarette smoke, from a habit which is excessively popular in this country. The language is lyrical, gentle, and replete with words that convey humility, gratitude, and grand acknowledgment to the one being addressed.

I stepped out of Narita International Airport with both wonder and trepidation. My daughter had been in Tokyo for exactly ten days to begin her junior year studying economics and Japanese abroad at Sophia University. She had left our home with symptoms of the typical summer stomach virus that many were having in our community. However, this malady worsened during her flight to Japan, and compounded with the jet lag, culture shock, and the airport's loss of her luggage, had made for a horrendous transition. Her e-mails were increasingly worrisome and depressive. When her phone was installed, I was greeted with a torrent of uncharacteristic sobs.

"Mom, I am so depressed that I cry every day. These spells can just hit anytime, and when I hold the tears in at school or on the subway, I can barely breathe by the time I arrive at my tiny apartment. I feel confined and lonely. There are only a few students here and I can't sleep or eat. My diarrhea is worse and I don't know what to eat. Everything is so expensive, and I feel so guilty when I try to eat in a restaurant and cannot finish my dish after a few bites. The Japanese people are not wasteful, and it is offensive to waste food, but I am too sick to take another morsel. I can't decide what to buy in the supermarket, so is it okay to eat Cocoa Crispies with milk for dinner?"

More sobs and my maternal heart was broken. Yet my psychiatrist's brain was quickly hearing the classic symptoms of a possible depression in just this one conversation: crying, insomnia, poor appetite, indecisiveness, poor concentration, and excessive guilt. When I questioned her further I discovered other signs that would total up to the nine or ten symptoms that define depression. She had excessive fatigue, pessimism or negative thinking, and anhedonia, which means loss of pleasure. The only two symptoms she did not have yet were bodily agitation or slowing and suicidal thoughts. If she had only five of these complaints for two weeks or more, she would be diagnosed with clinical depression in my office. I was not going to wait the two weeks for this to happen. I needed to address her physical illness, which I believed was causing all this, and to take care of her. Of course, I also had to bolster her spiritual condition, which was heroically strong as she clung onto God in her misery. She wanted desperately to find a church. She felt alone and thought she needed to talk to somebody, anybody, or everybody.

Alternatively, she also felt the desire to withdraw and talk to nobody. So this sad, much skinnier, but grateful young daughter of mine hugged me as I emerged from baggage claim and entered the land of the rising sun. Would I be facing the thunderstorms of my daughter's acculturation, or would there be showers of blessings on Genevieve and me? God is the great physician. This has been my stand in my medical career. I am just privileged to be his tool as he gives healing to the patients I treat. His healing extends from the many medicines he gives science and the many treatments or psychotherapy modalities that have value even if they are not perfect. Finally, his healing can be the result of a purely divine intervention and the answer to my fervent, consistent prayers on my patients' behalf. In talking to those who suffer, I ask God for his prescription for what to say as described in the book of Proverbs, "A word aptly spoken is like apples of gold in settings of silver." Combined with good listening skills, excellent care, and patience, the work of the Holy Spirit is the foundation for therapy. I call this the biopsychosociotheological model. Can I bring this framework to my daughter and add onto it the mother's nurturance, love, and care that I really wanted to deliver? The first two days I silenced my anxiety in order to listen so that she could have a chance to talk and ventilate all her unhappiness. I wanted her to know that I understood her suffering. She had been feeling like a failure in her adaptation because I had come to Japan.

She thought that maybe she should tough it out by herself. I reminded her that many parents accompany their children to college when they go away. My coming now did not reflect any inability on her part; I just had come a week later than most parents do. She had been so independent in her freshman and sophomore years at college that we had no doubt she could manage this educational experience without us, too. But we did not foresee her becoming ill at the point of departure. So in Tokyo, I cooked her favorite foods, which were now decidedly American: burgers, spaghetti and white clam sauce, and grilled salmon, because she was sickened at the thought of the Japanese foods she ordinarily craved—sushi, teriyaki, tonkatsu, etc. Her diarrhea persisted, and I reminded her that I would monitor it with her and take her to a doctor if the foods she was now eating did not help. The assurance that Mom was here to watch her gave her some peace of mind, but there was so much she had to obtain and do.

In order to continue her work in school she needed an electronic language dictionary, supplies for her apartment, and a bank to exchange our traveler's checks for currency. We found that to convert these checks to yen was not as easy as we had expected. It is very difficult to use any means of currency other than actual yen in Japan. Credit cards, American checks, and other monetary exchange items are not usable in many places, and she was frustrated with just trying to get money using her limited Japanese. She had encountered many rejections at stores and banks.

Finally, she needed a place to worship. Where does one go in a foreign land, and can the Lord show us even in this unfamiliar place? With only prayers of pleading, heavy hearts, and my own desire to be encouraging, we asked God to show us the way to find a Christian home for Gen the next day. That night, before she tried to go into her fitful sleep, she received an e-mail from Pastor Kim of the Shibuya Evangelical Church with an invitation and directions to go to their Sunday service. She called him on the phone and they decided that the evening service would be good for her, as English was spoken in addition to Japanese, catering to an international congregation. "By the way, Mom, he wanted to know if you would be the guest speaker tomorrow night," Gen said. "Tell him yes," I replied.

This unexpected request felt powerfully like an opportunity from God for which I did not have the option to hesitate. So while Gen slept, I prepared my talk, asking God for his direction and apt words for this congregation of people, all strangers to us. Pastor Kim was a colleague of friends of mine whom I had met during their time in the United States. A French pastor and his Japanese wife, JeanChristophe and Keiko, graciously made the connection for us from their home in Paris. They were very supportive of Genevieve and knew that her adjustment in the town of Heiwadai was extremely rough.

God used these dear people to find us a church at the zero hour. Evening service, also called Shibuya Harvest Ministry, was a pleasant worship experience complete with the familiar hymns and contemporary songs that Gen and I knew well from our home church. When alternating English with the Japanese verses, I heard the lovely voice of my daughter singing in both languages, and I knew that God was continuing to strengthen and teach her how to worship him in another tongue. Up to this point she had been too overwhelmed and anxious to use her junior high school level of Japanese that she had learned in the States, but the church service gave her an opportunity to sing the words in a safe place without recrimination or ridicule. Her voice, which she had "lost" from fear and weakness, became a little stronger.

After this I noticed she attempted to speak Japanese more often as the days went by. It was as if her tongue had been released from the paralyzing grip of anxiety through the praiseful singing.

What does a blind woman say in one hour (with Japanese translation) to a congregation of total strangers and her sad, worried, and still somewhat sick trooper of a daughter? Is there such a message that will convey hope to her, give the listeners a clear sense of God's strength, and provide scriptural wisdom to meet the many unknown cares of this audience? The answer was decidedly YES. Pastor Kim, with his kind, sensitive conversation with Gen in his office, ended our chat with a prayer for the evening's program, and I knew I was prepared to speak a message of love with my heart, mind, and soul.

My testimony that my blindness had come at just the time in my life to afford me the chance to leave my consuming OB/GYN residency and be a full-time mom, gave me the chance to tell my daughter how much I loved her and her brother. I said blindness was an answer to my prayer to be the primary nurturer and parent to them and that I considered it a gift from God. I said I would have never changed this life course even if I were given the hypothetical chance. Parenting them and being blind may seem to be bittersweet and contrasting developments, but in my case it was all for the good. The congregation heard about the moments and images I cherish in my mind's eye about those early years of my children's lives when I still had some sight left. I was hoping that Gen would hear that my love for her was a priority. She needed to know that putting all things aside to rush to her in Japan was but a small example of what a mother would gladly do, especially a mother who has seen that it is better to be blind and be with your children than to be sighted and practicing as a physician. Motherhood is a vocation or rather a privilege that only one person can fulfill and do wholeheartedly!

The second part of my message spoke of my wall-climbing episode, which illustrates the need for perseverance in the Christian life. It can be overwhelming, frightening, and exhausting at times, but clinging to faith is the essential ingredient to obtaining the goal. Could this encouragement be useful to the church members and would it address the issues that Gen was facing? The concluding segment was devoted to the seven coping skills for anxiety found in Philippians 4:6-9:

> *Do not be anxious about anything, but in every situation, by prayer and petition, with thanksgiving, present your re-*

quests to God. And the peace of God, which transcends all understanding, will guard your hearts and your minds in Christ Jesus. Finally, brothers and sisters, whatever is true, whatever is noble, whatever is right, whatever is pure, whatever is lovely, whatever is admirable—if anything is excellent or praiseworthy—think about such things. Whatever you have learned or received or heard from me, or seen in me— put it into practice. And the God of peace will be with you.

Slowly and steadily, I developed and repeated the seven steps in dealing with anxiety and worries that come from this passage. These seven directives also make up the basic principles of cognitive-behavioral therapy for anxiety disorders, and I have integrated them into my practice. The seven coping skills are as follows:

1. First, stop anxious thoughts. This is counterintuitive, as most people dwell on what worries them in order to find solutions. If it is a chronic worry, such preoccupation will only make it worse by sustaining the worry loop. Instead, individuals should find techniques and practices that work for them to nip worrisome thoughts in the bud. Some people snap rubber bands on their wrists to remind themselves to get away from an anxious thought. Others visualize a big stop sign, and others just tell themselves a determined "no."

2. Focus on something else. This could be another activity or, as stated in the book of Philippians, they could turn all their attention to God. The phrase "in everything" describes reshifting one's focus from worries to something else. What better focus can there be for a Christian than on the sovereign God who can provide comfort and aid?

3. Practice prayer and petition. This should not be limited to repetitive prayer about one's worry, as that would be analo-

gous to dwelling on the anxious thought. Rather, the individual should resume his or her normal prayer life of adoration, intercession, confession, and thanksgiving. The latter turns out to be the fourth coping skill.

4. Count Your Blessings. The mind can do only one thing at a time. If it is thinking about what one is thankful for, as in counting one's blessings, this will crowd out the worries. Because mood is dependent on thought in cognitive behavioral theory, thanksgiving can bring the mood from anxiety to calm and even joy.

5. Think about what is true and real. Many anxious people dwell on the worst-case scenario, with "what if" thoughts making these thoughts seem real when they are statistically unlikely. Although the worried individual knows that his or her thinking is not realistic, he or she feels as if the worst is likely to happen. God tells us to believe only that which is real and set our minds on it. He listed a host of other things for a person to set his or her mind on. One such item is to think about what is "lovely," which is the sixth coping skill, "visualization."

6. Visualize Your Favorite Places. In creation, God has given each one of us lovely scenes in our memory. Visualizing them by using our imagination to bring these scenes into our mind's eye for an interval of time can be relaxing and calming.

7. Practice These Skills Daily. Philippians 4:9 refers to the need to practice these seven skills daily, especially if we are prone to worry. One cannot give up after one try and say it does not work. The effectiveness of these skills comes only with a lifetime of practice. I reminded the audience that it will become easier with time and habitual repetition. The end result will be that God's peace will guard their hearts and

minds in Christ. With this prescription for anxiety, I ended my missive of a mother's love and motivational message for perseverance. It was my hope that these words would meet the needs of the congregation as well as my daughter.

After the service, Genevieve came up to me and told me she took notes on all the seven biblical coping skills for anxiety. "Great," I said. At this point, I wanted to stay by her side and facilitate her meeting others. I was concerned that in her condition she might be too withdrawn and shy, qualities previously unknown to this child who is very adept at meeting people and making friends. I did not want to be the center of attention, but soon I was inundated by people wishing to thank me, ask questions, or discuss their problems. As much as I struggled to stay by Gen's side, I was pulled away to speak privately to someone. I was torn because I wanted to be polite and sensitive, but my priority was to ease my daughter's entry into this fellowship.

When I quickly made my way back to the chapel, I was delighted to hear her conversing animatedly in English with some young people in the church. What a relief! This church was doing a lot of healing and good for Gen. Over the earlier course of the week Gen still had many sad and anxious periods during the day. Yet the fighter in her kept going to classes and forcing herself to eat the many things I prepared for her. Food shopping with the generous honorarium given to me by Pastor Kim symbolically showed her God's grace and generosity, especially since we still could not find a bank to get yen from our traveler's checks, and our own supply was low.

When she was indecisive about buying the expensive Japanese produce, I urged her to put any food that mildly appealed to her in the cart and told her not to worry about it, as she needed proper nutrition. She needed good food to counteract her illness which left her looking like Twiggy, the British model from a previous era. "Eating well now despite the expense is proper stewardship of the body God gave you," I admonished. We demonstrated hospitality to a classmate who lived in her apartment building. Gen wanted to "practice hospitality," as the Bible says, to this wonderful girl who had befriended her, and we then invited her to go shopping and spend some time with us. Besides her and the Shibuya young people, God started supplying new relationships that week, including an InterVarsity staff member; a visiting friend from California who spends holidays with family in Japan; Yumiko, a woman who I had taught when she was studying at Alliance Theological Seminary; and other foreign students in the building who had already spent time studying at Sophia University.

The ample provision of caring friends started to work to heal her withdrawn state. She started to regain her appetite and her sleep normalized. God also put us in front of a bank while we were shopping. We thought we had serendipitously found an open bank, so we walked in to inquire about exchanging traveler's checks for yen. Again they denied our request as had all the other banks we had visited, but they pointed us to one in the neighborhood that would help. It took us a while to find it, and I whispered a blind person's prayer: "Lord put our eyes on this place as we cannot tell where we are to go." Lo and behold, we were staring at a nonbank-like storefront which, to our amazement, was still open in the late afternoon. When they said they were willing to cash our $5,500 worth of traveler's checks, we broke out into a chorus of ecstasy and relief. It turns out that the bank's name included the surname of Yumiko's husband's corporate employer.

This lovely Christian couple had helped Gen settle into her apartment the previous week. We did not find this out until we met them for dinner later in the week. However, this was Wednesday, and when we returned home, ate dinner, and got ready for bed, I sensed something was dramatically different about Gen. She had eaten all of her dinner for the first time in many clays, and there was more. When she said her prayers that night, I could tell from the content that she had made the turn toward health.

It was clear to me as a mother and also a psychiatrist that a significant switch had occurred. My whole body flooded with release, and the tears just flowed into my eyes as I quickly finished my own "Amen" and kissed her goodnight. I had to run to the bathroom so I could cry freely for joy so as not to worry her.

As you would expect, Gen continued her recovery to health. By the time I left on Saturday, she was her usual self—the familiar confident, healthy, friendly young woman I knew. Even more, she had grown from this experience—wiser, with greater character, and with spiritual strength and the ability to weather hardship. She had a greater trust in God to help her through tough times.

Yumiko and her husband Masafumi told us about her 101-year-old grandfather who was still alive and well, living with his almost-centenarian wife of seventy-six years. She told of his sagacity and his calming influence on her and the lives of many others. People enjoyed being in his company. What does it take to have such blessings of character and longevity? The grandfather says one must be like the willow tree. If one studies it, one sees how it bends with the winds and the elements with ease and strength. It is its intrinsic flexibility that gives it the power to endure and remain strongly planted. In the same way, people must acquire the suppleness to bend with the winds of life's adversities in order to remain confident and planted in the place where they should be. Just live like the willow, and you will be not only strong but also calm and unfaltering under stress.

Yumiko has drawn a lot of strength from her grandfather's words. She and Masafumi themselves have gone through many transitions and hardships, and through culture shock, as they have had to live abroad in Singapore, in the United States, and now back in Japan. It is precisely the difficulties with these adjustments that made her a wonderful model and advisor to Gen in the first week. Gen had longed for Yumiko's company and conversation when she first arrived. Yumiko's grandfather teaches that if a person is climbing a mountain, he or she must have the faith to know it is done one step

> **Although the trail is long and the mountain dauntingly high, the climber must believe that at some point in the future he or she will be able to look back and see that the climb is complete.**

at a time. He or she must also believe that although the trail is long and the mountain dauntingly high, he or she must have the outlook that at some point in the future he or she will be able to look back and see that the climb is complete. We will see that we have overcome what we thought we could not do. We must be like the willow tree to have the hope of making it. Genevieve understood this teaching in a deeper way as the Tanis told us this story. She has a renewed outlook on her upcoming year in a foreign land. She e-mailed her dad back home and told him she was going to make it through the year now. As with my own life, God has transformed my daughter into the flourishing willow tree.

Blessed is the man who does not walk in the counsel of the wicked or stand in the way of sinners or sit in the seat of mockers. But his delight is in the law of the LORD, and on his law he meditates day and night. He is like a tree planted by streams of water, which yields its fruit in season and whose leaf does not wither. Whatever he does prospers (Psalm 1:1-3).

Questions for personal consideration and/or group discussion:

1. What do you think of the biopsychsociotheological model of counseling?

    ___ It considers all arenas of a person's life

    ___ It frees me to look beyond the typical psychological arenas in order to get to the heart of a person's problem

    ___ It's hard for me to focus on all these arenas at one time with each person

    ___ It's difficult to process all these factors, in my own life and also the lives of others.

2. How did you feel about the statement "blindness as an answer to prayer, and a gift from God"? Further, how does this statement affect you: "I would have never changed this life course even if given the hypothetical chance to do so."

    How might you go about helping a disabled person to adopt this point of view? What would you call this point of view?

3. The seven steps in dealing with anxiety, based on Philippians 4:6-9 are:

    a. Stop anxious thoughts

    b. Focus on something else

    c. Practice prayer and petition

    d. Count your blessings

    e. Think about what is true and real

    f. Visualize your favorite places

    g. Practice these skills daily

Which of these has been most difficult for you to practice, yourself?

Which of these has been most difficult for others to adopt?

Is this really an antidote for anxiety, or just a few words of exhortation from a guy named Paul?

4. Yumiko's grandfather said that we must be like a willow tree, bending with the winds and the elements with ease and strength. Its intrinsic flexibility gives it the power to endure and remain strongly planted. Similarly, we must acquire the suppleness to bend with life's adversities, unfaltering under stress.

What Scripture passages or teachings does this teaching bring to mind?

Are you like a willow, or more like trees that break when the elements are harsh?

How can you help your others adopt attitudes that will make them more resilient?

For You formed my inward parts; You covered me in my mother's womb. I will praise You, for I am fearfully and wonderfully made; Marvelous are Your works, and that my soul knows very well. My frame was not hidden from You, when I was made in secret, and skillfully wrought in the lowest parts of the earth. Your eyes saw my substance, being yet unformed. And in Your book they all were written, the days fashioned for me, when as yet there were none of them.

Psalm 139: 13-16, NKJV

Chapter 5

Resolve in Real Time: One Doctor's Story

It's been my privilege to support Christian doctors whose life experience has uniquely prepared them for medical service in the name of the Great Physician, Jesus. One such doctor in training is T.S. We met through the Director of the Health Center where she volunteered. We had an immediate connection due to our immersion in the question of loss as we made our way along the pathway we believed God had established for us.

Dr. S. was shell-shocked by the system (and also by her life experiences) when we first met. She was a person resolved to follow God's leading, but due to multiple rejections, she wasn't as confident as she might have been that her experiences over a number of years had uniquely prepared her to practice medicine in the field of Child and Adolescent Psychiatry. She seemed worried, as was reasonable, that the "gaps" in her training had rendered her inadequate to handle the load ahead. She knew in her heart that she was prepared to do Child Psychiatry, but she didn't know if anyone else would see that in her and give her a chance. I told her, "I meet a lot of psychiatric residents who really don't know much about life—I mean life the way it can be in the trenches. As I see it, you are ahead of the game, and the perceived 'gap' in your training is irrelevant."

From the moment I met Dr. S., I could see that she would be perfect for a position with me as a Medical and Mental Health Educational Associate at the Christian Graduate School for counseling where I teach. I was impressed with her focus on her son's needs (when so many doctors in training ignore their families) and also with her immediate interest in learning to practice psychiatry from a Christian perspective.

Treating the whole person—body, mind, and spirit—has been my practice commitment since I retrained in psychiatry, and it was clear that she understood this perspective, including our need to practice self-care in order to responsibly treat patients in a truly holistic sense.

It was wonderful to see the transformation that occurred once Dr. S. was free of the highly stressful and competitive secular training programs she had been pursuing, and in a position where she did not have to fight for approval or respect. Our local community of Christian physicians who are members of the Christian Medical & Dental Associations provided a significant level of support for her and she resolutely followed her calling to care for those who are experiencing some of the same issues that she has faced.

Because her story is so unique and inspirational, I asked her to share it with you so you can see what resolve looks like in real time in a real world setting:

I was born in India and was brought to the United States when I was four years old. My father was the pastor of a church that sought to provide a Christian community for Tamil-speaking people in the U.S. My parents were dedicated to this work even though they had other full-time jobs to provide for our family. They were loving and supportive to me and my older brother. As a child, I remember wondering why anyone would have family problems; from my perspective, it was so easy! I thought that I could be anything. I had big dreams of having a successful career, a happy family, plenty of money, and a great reputation as an upstanding Christian woman in my community. I was confident that I could achieve all of this by the age of twenty-five. Clearly, God had other plans for me that I could not appreciate until many years later.

My father passed away when I was twelve years old. I lost my best cheerleader in life; he was always proud of me and he believed that I would do great things. It was a major loss but I had such a strong support system in the rest of my family and church friends that I did not fully understand what I missed until I was in college. A more immediate effect of losing my beloved father and pastor of my church was that I evaluated my faith more critically. I was at the age when children in my church typically went through a ceremony to publicly declare that they are owning the faith in which they were raised. I delayed my confirmation because I had asked the Lord to show me without any doubt that he was real. As an adolescent, my prayer was still not answered but I was confirmed anyway. I didn't know for certain that God was real but I also couldn't imagine denying my faith. I reasoned that, perhaps, this is the best that I can know God. This type of relationship with God did not inspire me to pursue him more intently, so I focused my attention on academics through the high school and undergraduate years. However, the Lord was faithful to answer my prayer eleven years later while I was in a graduate program for neuroscience at a large university. Until then, I didn't know that I could have an intimate relationship with God in which he gives me practical guidance for every day and he expresses his love for me in tangible ways.

Of note, this revelation came at a time when my perfect family was not so perfect. I didn't feel fully supported by my family because they had their own problems. My friends in the graduate program were also moving in different directions so I could no longer count on them. The lack of support caused me to question the purpose of my life. Why should I work so hard to be a good person or to be successful? What difference does it make if I live life well or not? Who cares about me? I asked God for an intimate relationship with him like the one he had with my housemate. The Lord used the little faith I had to ask him for intimacy in the midst of this situation to show me that he is the source of the kind of love and support that I'd been longing to have. My circumstances did not improve during this time but I was full of joy because God's love and support for me was tangible. Moreover, I understood that he had a purpose for my life before I was created in the womb:

> *For You formed my inward parts; You covered me in my mother's womb. I will praise You, for I am fearfully and wonderfully made; Marvelous are Your works, and that my soul knows very well. My frame was not hidden from You, when I was made in secret, and skillfully wrought in the lowest parts of the earth. Your eyes saw my substance, being yet unformed. And in Your book they all were written, the days fashioned for me, when as yet there were none of them* (Psalm 139: 13-16, NKJV).

I was surrounded by other Christians who helped me to grow in my faith. As we read and discussed Bible passages, I realized that God's Word has a lot to say about how I live every day. The Bible came alive to me as a way for God to communicate with me. When I read verses that were relevant to what I faced, I was excited to apply the principles and see the positive effects. One of my friends took me shopping to select a daily devotional; for months, that devotional had a Bible passage and a few paragraphs of discussion on the very thing that I was most concerned about that day. People who had gone away for the summer could see the positive transformation in my character when they returned. My friends also had me taking on small leadership roles like leading a small Bible study group in my house every morning; this pushed me to pray for the others in the group and to ask God for direction. When God wanted me to do something that was outside of my comfort zone like share a particular testimony, the Holy Spirit would give me a strong nudge; I never regretted following these promptings. Even though I wasn't right all the time, I was learning how to hear from God. Later on I learned that I don't need to be concerned that I'm not perfect because God always works in and through imperfect people to accomplish his plan and purpose. In any case, I had the assurance from Romans 8:28 that "in all things God works for the good of those who love him, who have been called according to his purpose."

While I was building a solid foundation in my faith for five years, I was also nearing the completion of my doctoral degree in neuroscience. This is when my thesis advisor, Dr. Norma, finally lost her battle with an aggressive form of ovarian cancer. Norma's love and dedication for research echoed that of my parents for the ministry. I'll never forget watching Dr. Norma's husband bringing her into the lab in a wheelchair. She had lost about thirty pounds and she had a bag of ascites fluid draining from her abdomen. She just came in to check her mail and to see how I was progressing. Dr. Norma got her PhD after she had finished raising her twin daughters. My parents and Dr. Norma modeled for me the great satisfaction in doing something you love even if you have to wait until later in life. They also demonstrated that there are ways to enjoy a wonderful career and family.

Dr. Norma's death was life-altering for me. Because research projects at the doctoral level are highly specialized, the expertise and the dedicated funding provided by my thesis advisor made her uniquely qualified to help me complete my degree. I had four difficult options before me, but I can see now that God prepared me with just the right kind of life experience and faith in him to make a wise decision. Option 1: Change my project significantly in order to satisfy the remaining professors in the department who all had an engineering background. I wasn't really equipped or interested in making such changes especially since this would be the basis for the kind of work I would do after graduation. Option 2: Start from scratch in a new university with a professor whose research was similar to mine. Option 3: Pursue a different career. Option 4: Get married and raise children instead of focusing on my career.

After seeking guidance from the Lord, I decided to change careers. I had been interested in pursuing medicine for years but, when I had been offered a position in the doctoral program, I thought it was a perfectly good alternative. I believe that I had a God-given desire in my heart to become a physician but he was in no hurry to make this happen. He was more interested in shaping my character and developing my relationship with him than he was in meeting deadlines that I had made for myself.

The apostle Paul wrote, "And I am certain that God, who began the good work within you, will continue his work until it is finally finished on the day when Christ Jesus returns" (Philippians 1:6, NLT). There is risk involved with spending precious time and money to pursue a highly-competitive, lengthy, and intensive training program during the time when I should be thinking about starting a family and caring for my aging mom. In the two years that it took for me to prepare my application for medical school, the Lord confirmed to me time and time and time again that this was his plan; as I later learned, he had a purpose in hammering this concept into my head.

There were several obstacles ahead of me that I would have to overcome. Would I have my mom's support when family and friends were saying that, at my age, I should just finish whatever I started, get married, and take care of my widowed mother? Would any medical school consider me with an incomplete PhD after studying for so many years? How would I manage the delay in starting a family? Here are just a few ways in which he reassured me. First of all, Dr. Norma supported my decision by writing a strong letter of recommendation for me just before she died. My new advisor also wrote a letter and gave me two months of paid time off to study for the medical school entrance exam. I received this favor in a department that typically saw medicine as a second tier option compared to scientific research in a large university.

Secondly, my mother found God-given strength to conceal from me her new cancer diagnosis and months of chemotherapy treatment. Even though she was living alone and needed support, she chose to show her support for my decision by protecting my study time. God showed me that he would provide for her as I followed his leading; she has been cancer-free following treatment.

Thirdly, he gave me favor in the eyes of a medical school dean who encouraged me to apply to medical school and helped me with the application process; he was a former colleague of Dr. Norma.

Fourthly, as I waited for responses from medical schools, I was uncertain if I had heard from God correctly. It didn't help that family and friends questioned my motives. They would say:

> "She says she's following God's will for her life? That's just a convenient excuse to set aside her responsibilities and do whatever she wants."

> "Just finish studying and get married before you get too old to find a good partner. You need to take care of your mother now."

It was then that God reassured me with this Scripture: "When He opens doors, no one will be able to close them; when He closes doors, no one will be able to open them" (Isaiah 22:22, NLT).

Then I was able to trust him no matter what the outcome.

Even after God settled my mind that the outcome was in his hands, I was still itching to know the answer so that I could confidently press toward that goal without wasting my time. But God used the time of uncertainty to motivate me to turn to him more intently. It also protected me from being overwhelmed by all that was ahead of me. I could not have appreciated the treasures that were in store for me as I endured hard times. As the Scripture says: "For I know the plans I have for you," declares the Lord, "plans to prosper you and not to harm you, plans to give you hope and a future" (Jeremiah 29:11). He has been masterfully using the good and bad circumstances in my life to prepare me to fulfill those plans with him. He's been careful to stretch and grow my faith in him without breaking my resolve.

When I finally got my acceptance letter from SUNY Upstate Medical University, I praised the Lord for the answered prayer and for what I had learned in the process. I thought that the hardest part was over and that the rest of my life would be more straightforward. However, I found my medical school years to be demanding both in and out of school. For instance, there seemed to be a constant stream of potential marriage partners that I was expected to consider because they came from the same part of India, had a good job, came from a decent family, and identified as Christians. I wanted someone who had also discovered this wonderful relationship with God like I had because it would strongly influence our perspectives and decisions as a couple.

We were not able to find the man who met all the requirements so this became a source of stress. Adding a few stressors like this to a full course load was proving to be a challenge. One of my medical school deans suggested that I take a year off since I had so much on my plate. Since I couldn't clearly identify the root of my problem or a solution, I didn't see the point of delaying my training even further and enduring criticism for "wasting my time at home when I should be studying." I felt like my life was a moving train with mechanical difficulties that could not be stopped for anything short of a miracle or death. Well-meaning advisors misunderstood and minimized my painful experiences; they were not equipped to help me through it.

    I graduated from medical school with a great testimony of God's faithfulness to me and I started pediatric residency in a reputable program. I had hoped that this would be a fresh start for me, but the unresolved issues continued to affect me in the new setting. God knew the drastic changes ahead of me would give me the much-needed opportunity to slow down, reflect, and heal. He was developing my character, my compassion for people, and my understanding of his love and commitment to me. He was equipping me with the essentials for having the abundant, fulfilling life that God promises and that we all long to have. It was hard to fully appreciate all this good because it often came through so much pain and suffering. However, God has helped me to focus more on his perspective, which is full of hope and joy, and less on my old default perspective, which was full of negativity. I used to think that the negativity was a natural outflow of the negative circumstances I faced. Now I know that my circumstances do not have to dictate how I think and how I respond.

    In the middle of my second year of residency training, I was diagnosed with clinical depression. I didn't positively identify it in medical school because I reasoned that anyone in my stressful situation might respond this way. I was also pretty good at addressing symptoms by looking to the Bible, sermons online, elders in the church, prayer, worship, etc. God provided a wonderful study partner and friend in medical school to keep up with my studies. But this wasn't the complete solution because I still had times when I wasn't able to function as I should have. The issue was exacerbated in residency by the expectation to perform at a higher level and by the unrelenting outside pressures. My relief from this issue was delayed, because it took many months to find a well-trained and supportive psychiatrist. In the interim, I was not improving and no one, including myself, knew the reason. So the working assumption by my residency program director was that I didn't have the character to be in medicine.

In my mind, I had big dreams and good intentions but doubted I was good enough at executing any of it. I thought I was a failure in my profession since my best efforts at work were inadequate. I thought I was a failure in my family life since I couldn't financially support my mom or get married. I even thought I was a failure before God because I didn't do my part toward fulfilling his plans for my life; I felt condemned when I read some of the conditional promises in the Bible. I often asked God to take my life since everything was so messed up and I thought my life had minimal value for others. I would have been completely hopeless except I had walked too far with God to deny that he was real and I knew that he was able to guide me through this situation. Having said that, I also wondered how much lower he would allow me to fall before he rescued me. It all seemed unbearable but, as I continued to look to him, he helped me to endure by providing the encouragement and hope I needed to keep going.

Because of the lack of understanding of this diagnosis in the Indian culture, in many churches, as well as in the medical field, I didn't know who I could trust to help me. Moreover, I was already having a hard time with my own negative thoughts so I didn't need others to make it worse. Eventually, when the news got out, I was criticized and written off by those around me:

> "She's not depressed. She's just saying that because she is struggling in her residency program."

> "You shouldn't be depressed if your faith and trust in God is strong enough."

> "She's not depressed. She was smiling that day when we visited her. She just needs to toughen up."

"Her problems are not that bad. I had similar problems and I handled it just fine."

"All she has to do is pop a pill and show up at a therapist's office regularly. If she can't do that, it's because she's not really dedicated to doing what she needs to be a good physician. She shouldn't be in medicine."

"Depression is not a real illness; she's just weak."

In addition, people kept their distance because there is a pervasive stigma associated with any mental illness.

Just before I was diagnosed with depression, a relationship was developing with my future husband who we'll call Sanjiv; he brought me happiness in the midst of all the stress. He became the only person who I felt comfortable sharing what I was facing. I felt peace in my heart that this was the kind of man I had waited for all these years. He was an Indian Christian man who had overcome significant challenges in his own life. I thought that it was this life experience that helped him to see the value in me despite my circumstances at the time. Sanjiv worked in Christian

> **Because of the lack of understanding of clinical depression in my native Indian culture, in many churches, as well as in the medical field, I didn't know who I could trust to help me.**

organizations with widely-respected leaders who vouched for his character after living with him and working closely with him. He was so understanding and good throughout our courtship. Sanjiv and I had similar values and compatible goals for the future. We had great conversations that could last for hours. Sanjiv was finishing his MBA at a Christian university so his income was limited but he was so generous in spending his money on what he thought would please me. He had a prayer partner who met with him regularly for two years just to pray for a future wife; they were so thrilled that I was the answer to his prayers. No matter what time I was going to work or coming home, he was ready to start and end his day with me. If things didn't go his way, he seemed to be an easy-going kind of guy who had overcome too much in his life to let those little things bother him. I thought that Sanjiv was sent by the Lord just in time to stand with me during this dark time and our relationship would mark the beginning of our bright future together.

Soon after Sanjiv and I were married, I got the dreaded news that the residency program had decided not to renew my contract but they would allow me to keep working that year for a salary. Weeks later, we were asked to move out of our apartment on short notice. We found a lovely new apartment which was flooded with water just after we moved in. I was still working eighty hours a week. Needless to say, it was a stressful time. A couple of months later, I was introduced by my clinic supervisor to the psychiatrist I still see today. She appreciated how well I was functioning despite the obstacles. Within three short months of treatment, I was no longer clinically depressed. She advocated for me to return to my old program, but it was a closed door.

After a few more months, while I was not working and preparing for my next steps, my husband and I decided that this was a good a time as any to have a child. We were not getting any younger and being pregnant in a new residency program wasn't going to be any easier. I suffered from complications in my pregnancy such as severe nausea until the end of the second trimester, exhaustion, gestational diabetes as well as returning symptoms of depression with the hormonal changes. I needed more recovery time to be mentally prepared to face the demands of a new program. As we faced multiple stressors, the godly man I thought I married became progressively more abusive to the point at which safety became the highest priority. Verbal abuse with cursing, criticism, lying, manipulation, controlling and demeaning words worsened to breaking larger and larger objects in anger and aggression toward me.

Added to this was physical abuse followed by threats if I were to seek help from anyone. No family, friends, or church members held him accountable for his actions. No one was there to protect me and my baby. In fact, many people couldn't accept that Sanjiv grossly mistreated his family because he has worked so hard to manipulate people's perceptions of himself. When we were well into our marriage, he admitted to me that the man I saw behind closed doors was the real Sanjiv but he was not about to fully reveal it to others. Later, through much study on domestic violence, I have come to understand that the real Sanjiv is deeply damaged by the events and people in his past. He is in bondage to the fear of facing his awful past with a trustworthy counselor. As a result, our family lives with the consequences of his unhealed wounds. I have empathy for his position but separation is necessary for our survival and to provide him with the accountability he needs.

I spent many hours as a pregnant woman convincing myself that life is worth living even though my unborn baby and I were in an environment that was a set-up for disaster. What I really wanted at that time was to have the kind of validation and support that I didn't get until later. In the interim, I was learning to trust in the character of God and to wait for him to work all things together for good for me and my child as he promised in the Bible. Despite the problems, I was a joyful expectant mother. Even though my husband didn't acknowledge it, I felt more beautiful than I had at any other time as a woman. I delivered my beautiful, healthy baby boy who we'll call Joshua. He has been supernaturally protected and given great favor in the eyes of God and man in the midst of the storm-filled family into which he was born. By the grace of God, I was no longer depressed once I delivered Joshua. I believe this was because I was no longer influenced by the hormonal changes of pregnancy and because I was emboldened to protect my son and to be the best mother I could be for him.

My mother invited us to live with her when our son was born; this eased the financial pressure and provided a measure of protection just in case. The abuse worsened to the point that my mother often confined herself to the bedroom of her own home to avoid Sanjiv. I could see the beginnings of the same escalating pattern of abuse with our son. When I warned Sanjiv that I would call the police next time he physically abused me, he threatened that he would take "the kid" away from me by saying that I was too depressed to competently care for him. I was very careful not to let Sanjiv watch Joshua any longer than he wanted lest it trigger some abusive behavior. When I had a large bruise on my arm after being beaten in the presence of my newborn baby, I sought help to no avail from our pastor, a Christian marriage and family therapist, and a few people whom my husband respected.

I decided to change my approach because I found that there was a worsening atmosphere of fear and intimidation in my home. My interventions within the family and the church were clearly ineffective. God provided me with time to study the Bible and go through various teachings on dysfunctional families and domestic violence. God provided wise counsel to thoughtfully develop a safety plan. I would never have had the time to do this if I were in a residency program. In fact, the combination of pressure to excel in a second residency program, care for a baby, and deal with domestic violence could have been disastrous. When my son was nine months old, it was clear that we needed to obtain an order of protection from the court to keep Sanjiv away from me and Joshua. Just as my friends prayed while I was in the court hearing, the truth came out as a result of my husband's own testimony. This step was not taken lightly because, unless there was a significant change in my husband, I knew that it would lead to the end of our marriage.

The victory was bittersweet because it was just the beginning of years in court for child custody and visitation schedules in a court system that values maintaining the parental rights of abusive parents more than it values the safety of children. My decision to separate from my husband because of abuse also led to the loss of my existing local social support system as well as the support of extended family members. While I was being vigilant about the possible violent backlash from my husband, he was trying to elicit sympathy from everyone on my contact list so that they could influence me to remove the order of protection and take him back. In my limited interactions with my husband, it was very clear that he was not safe to take back. Working through the imperfect court system was the best approach in our case.

It was disheartening to know that there were so many people in the background making judgments as they heard the latest news about me. They didn't understand the seriousness of the matter. From my perspective, I couldn't see how I could make it without the support of some of these people. It reminded me of Gideon's story in the Bible. God asked him to send home 31,700 soldiers who were less-than-ideal for a battle. This left him with only 300 soldiers. In the eyes of man, it seemed like an insufficient army, but God proved that he could be trusted to know how to gain the victory.

For a few months, I had no one. God used this time to establish his love and care for me and his all-sufficiency to provide for me. He would raise up just the right kind of people, even for limited periods of time, to help us through crucial times when we couldn't make it alone. Over the years, he has been slowly bringing wonderful new people across my path. It's not the same as having a spouse or a family member you can count on, but it has pushed me to depend on God and he has proved to be trustworthy.

One such amazing person brought by God was a Christian counselor who faithfully counseled me every week without expecting anything in return. She was a professor of Biblical Counseling who had been seasoned by decades of experience with abusive relationships. It felt so wonderful to have a caring professional validate the experiences that so many underestimated. Her words brought encouragement, godly wisdom, truth, and compassion. She always prayed with me because she knew that my life was in his hands. My psychiatrist was able to handle the medical component but my counselor pointed me to God who handles the lifelong process of healing and transformation.

I prayed for very limited contact with Sanjiv because it seemed to be the best way to stay safe, have peace, and get back on our feet. In his wisdom, God did not remove my husband but he did provide a measure of protection for us. Overall, my five-year-old son is a bright, happy, and well-adjusted little boy. He believes his father loves him and is proud of him which is very important for healthy development. I am entrusting whatever I can't see to God who can either completely shield Joshua from harm or he can redeem the pain. Unfortunately, the court's methods of looking for signs of abuse are not very effective unless it is blatantly obvious. The psychologist who monitored hour-long visits with my husband and son wrote glowing reports about my husband. The forensic psychologist who evaluated us agreed that my husband was not safe. However, he would not say that in his report because, "That's not what the courts want to hear and I need future referrals for myself." So he gave three months of court-ordered anger management and parenting classes instead. The child protective services spent more time evaluating me because I had a history of depression; they saw concerning things about my husband, but the system is not designed to pursue them so no one did anything. The lawyer assigned to Joshua to protect him believed that these interventions were all that the court could do; she could not understand why my husband didn't have full privileges as a parent. My husband's lawyer said that she beat her child with a stick until it broke. She said her child is fine, so why am I making a big deal about my situation? She pushed my husband to ask for joint custody and lots of visits with Joshua.

The court saw my husband as "healed" even though my interactions with him showed an unrepentant, and therefore unsafe, person who knew how to restore his reputation through deceiving others. I couldn't eat or sleep for weeks at the thought of spending longer periods of time with this man. I tried my best to keep the rush of thoughts and feelings under control by choosing a godly perspective and to praise God. On the morning of our court date, I got this verse in my spirit as I was driving Joshua to daycare, "Stand still and see the salvation of the Lord." From experience, I know it was God speaking to me.

As confirmation, my devotional reading for that day was on the very same verse. When I walked into the court house, everything unraveled before my eyes; I literally stood still and watched how God worked in their minds to give us the victory. My husband could not continue his job with an unsettled visa status. In the end, he and his lawyer reasoned that he had no choice but to concede sole custody of Joshua with no more visits than he already had. God was teaching me that he is sovereign. All the ignorance and the unjust circumstances that I thought were going to adversely affect the outcome were rendered irrelevant because my husband and I came to an agreement without a court hearing. Almighty God was taking care of me and my son so I was ready to move forward.

Now that the court cases were less frequent, I began one of many attempts to study for the board exam to get my medical license; I invested in daycare so that I would have some time for this intensive study schedule. During this time, my mother was offered a deal by developers to sell her home. As my mother was no longer able to maintain the home, it was an offer we couldn't afford to turn down. Because the deal was time sensitive, I had to set aside my studies and look for a new home in our highly-competitive housing market. My mom's home had accumulated thirty years of treasures from the previous owner and another twenty-three years of treasures from us. I was still "shunned" by our community so it was a monumental task for a single parent with an elderly mom who found it very difficult to make this change. However, God gave us supernatural favor with a large group of church members and he gave me supernatural ability to manage the 1.5 year moving process. There was a steady stream of opposition for all these changes but, in the end, this decision has given us the measure of stability that was needed through the years as I worked to regain a career.

After three years of stabilizing myself and my family, I was finally ready to return to a pediatric residency program. I knew that my experiences would make me a better physician than when I was fresh out of medical school. My character had been strengthened through all the difficult years. I had even been free of clinical depression since I delivered Joshua even though I faced challenges that were more difficult than ever. I had a dream interview in a hospital near my mom's home. I was so excited about the prospects, but it turned out to be a closed door because of the lack of support from my old program leadership. It was so discouraging to have gone through the year-long application process on top of everything else only to find that this obstacle could destroy any chance of residency for me.

I believe God gave me favor with an influential pediatric cardiologist who spoke to program directors on my behalf; she made these connections without even meeting me in person. We concluded that I would need to get a strong recommendation from a current full-time employer. There were constraints of location and time due to my family responsibilities, child visitation, and court cases. I needed an employer to be impressed with me in a short period and willing to recommend that I pursue another field. The field in which I worked should complement my interest in medicine. If I moved away from home, I needed to have an adequate salary to support a separate living space.

After eight months of faithful searching, I was not able to find the right job and unsure about how to proceed. Application season was around the corner and I had nothing to show for all my efforts. I questioned whether I should just give up on medicine; maybe God was closing the door to completing my training and he had something else for me. Practically speaking, I also had to consider a job that paid well enough to survive with massive student loans, possible attorney fees down the road, and supporting a child and an aging mom.

When I was tapped out of ideas, God brought into my life a childhood family friend who became a life coach. She offered to help me reassess my life free of charge. She believed that I had a bright and fulfilling future even though many continued to criticize me for not taking any opportunity to stand on my own feet. In light of my heart, my personality, and my experiences, I concluded that Child Psychiatry would be an even better fit for me than Pediatrics. Child Psychiatry allows me to focus on the aspects of Pediatrics which I enjoyed the most. I can spend more time listening to my patients and their families. I can positively impact the course of my patients' lives through early diagnosis and management. I get to benefit others with the understanding and compassion that I've gained by overcoming many challenges in life. I can use my position to advocate for abused and mentally ill in the hospitals, the church, and in the courts. In addition, the lifestyle of a psychiatrist is better for a single parent.

Child Psychiatry felt so right, but I knew that there were multiple miracles needed to make this a reality. Psychiatry residency is much more competitive than Pediatrics. I needed the help of a personal contact to even get a pediatric residency interview. I needed some family support to pursue a specialty with an associated stigma. I needed work experience in this field so I could get a strong letter of recommendation in time for application season. I needed my old program leadership to write a letter that would not sabotage my application. I needed to pass my board exam to enhance my application; this required at least three solid months of peaceful study time from waking to sleeping in order to prepare adequately; this was not possible with my family situation. After submitting my application, I needed the favor of residency programs to get interviews. Once I secured the residency position, I would need to conclude the court cases and to work out a reasonable visitation schedule with my husband. I would also need affordable and reliable child care as well as mom care. This was a tall order.

I tried studying for months while my son was in daycare, but it was clear that I needed even more time each day. As this exam was getting delayed, I thought that I should at least try to get some experience in the field of psychiatry but this was also not happening. In the interim, there was mounting pressure from people to abandon this plan completely. I was so desperate for work, I considered taking the required job assigned to people who get public assistance; a family friend wisely advised me that this would make it harder to study and the public assistance job would not really enhance my application. I struggled for another eight months.

At a low point, I started attending a women's Bible study in my church. The leader gave me a Word from the Lord that was so encouraging and refreshing. I learned that it was not uncommon for God to use struggles like mine to strengthen and prepare us for his great plans. Soon after, I found a great psychiatry externship opportunity that was minutes from my home. My application, which normally took months to prepare, was completed within a few days to meet the deadline. The interview appeared to go well but it was another closed door! This time I was able to quickly take on the perspective that God must have a better plan.

When residency application season came, Dr. Eng wrote me a very strong letter of recommendation. I even got a supportive letter from a key person in my old program leadership. My job with

Dr. Eng began after I took an intensive prep course for the medical licensing exam. The prep course is expensive and it's only offered once a year in our area. God gave me timely favor in the eyes of a family friend who offered to pay for the course and even for related child care expenses. The course offered teaching that I couldn't have obtained from a review book. As I met other students, I knew that I was not alone in my struggle to study and find work experience. Months later, I was able to take the exam and pass it.

The very next day, I received final divorce papers in the mail from my husband. So the marriage ended without my knowledge of the court date and without even signing papers. The way it happened was disconcerting at first, but I was relieved that this matter was concluded. One month later, I was invited for a residency interview. I had been introduced to the head of the department months before. She believed in me from the first time we met; God provided a strong advocate for me within the program. On interview day, I just told my story without having to fight to be understood. All four interviewers understood how beautifully prepared I was to pursue Child Psychiatry and they all appeared eager to accept me into their program. I walked away feeling so confident but I left room for the possibility that God was going to close this door as well. There were 2000 applicants for six available positions that year. A few months later, I received a phone call from the program director inviting me to accept a position in the program! In a short time, I watched as major obstacles were being removed and God was beginning to give me the long-standing desires of my heart.

Questions for personal consideration and/or group discussion:

1. Describe in five words or less your first reaction after reading this chapter.

2. What do you think of this statement: "He (God) was more interested in shaping my character and developing my relationship with him than he was in meeting deadlines that I had made for myself."

3. Put yourself into this story: How would you have handled all the obstacles and the waiting? How can you develop more patience?

4. Can you identify with the following statement? "I felt like my life was a moving train with mechanical difficulties that could not be stopped for anything short of a miracle or death." If you have felt this way, how did you move beyond this perspective?

5. Relationships can be toxic, but outsiders may not understand (or care to). Was this doctor justified in her actions? How would you advise her if she asked for your help?

6. What do you think kept her moving ahead?

> *If I speak in the tongues of men
> or of angels, but do not have love,
> I am only a resounding gong
> or a clanging cymbal.*
>
> 1 Corinthians 13:1

Chapter 6

Three Children of Honduras

Each day hundreds of young children are crossing the border, trying desperately to leave Central America and enter the U.S. Who are these unaccompanied minors, so desperate to escape their homeland, and why?

Jenny, a young college graduate, relocated to Honduras several years ago in order to share her faith and love with these children. Many of them are left alone in their home while their parents, if they still are around, eke out a meager living in one of the poorest countries in the world. Many have been abandoned to their "abuelos" (grandparents) or some other caretaker by parents who have either left the country, have been incarcerated, or killed.

Jenny, quiet and serious, stands contrastingly in her statuesque six-foot frame, working to teach and feed young ones, and now helping her Honduran husband to build a new school building for the children in Los Pinos. The couple faces the challenge of the enormous social, physical, and spiritual needs of these mountain dwellers.

José visited me in the makeshift medical clinic at the Rock church complaining of "dolor de estomago" (pain in the stomach). Rusty

> At 11:00 the gnawing hunger pains prey on José as he faces with uncertainty the origins of his next meal. I "treated" him for his malady from my own five-pound supply of peanuts in their shells.

in the practice of primary care medicine from a twenty-five-year career in psychiatry, I grappled with the differential diagnosis in the cause of his pain. Could this little eight-year-old boy have a case of hookworm, bacterial gastroenteritis, a brewing appendicitis, or the effects of food and water contamination that seem to be affecting many in the community? Entering into a prolonged conversation with this polite young boy, I learned the source of his pain. José told me that he had received the medication for worms in school a month ago and did not feel he was infected anymore. He did not have fever, diarrhea, or other symptoms. But he observed that he gets a lot of these stomach pains when he is hungry, a fact that occurs on a daily basis. His customary breakfast, proffered by his busy mother as she hurries to work is a cup of black coffee and a small piece of sweetened bread. At 11:00, the gnawing hunger pains prey on the youngster as he faces with uncertainty the origins of his next meal. As I "treated" him for his malady from my own five-pound supply of peanuts in their shells ("cacahuate") I lamented the fact that I did not bring a 100 pound bag to feed the line of children I knew would file into the clinic that week. What a pleasant surprise to see their genuine gratefulness as they received the "cacahuate" and what pain to see their quiet acceptance when they were told there was no more. Maybe they would not be running away from their Honduran homes if their stomachs were not so empty.

Esteban, a thirteen-year-old, was "an anger management" problem. Aben, Jenny's husband, asked if I could intervene. "May I speak to his parents," I asked?

"Not likely or possible," was the reply. That morning, J-nathan, the teacher assigned to monitor Esteban said Esteban was "tranquilo" (calm). We both agreed to leave him alone. Quite by accident, I bumped into Esteban on the soccer field. He told me he lived with his grandmother and his brothers, not mentioning his parents as if their absence was a norm. Esteban complained bitterly about his epileptic seizures, "attacks" which he believes make him unable to recall anger episodes. Yet he did not find it problematic that he often forgets to take the medication to control the attacks.

"Could anyone help you remember?" I asked. "Yes, I can ask my grandmother and cousins to make sure I take it," he replied.

Two days later he showed up at the medical clinic holding out a very bruised and swollen hand, which he had used to punch his brother the night before. His brother hangs out a lot around the neighborhood with the wrong types and had chosen to deride his epileptic brother in the presence of a friend. So much for anger management. How do you tell someone to control his anger when those in his environment deliberately provoke him to defend himself? In light of the absent parents and a grandmother who works six days a week, who could blame Esteban for being furious when so helpless. Nor could anyone blame him should he want to join a gang for protection. Fortunately, the Rock church and the ex-gang member, J-nathan, who takes great care to supervise and instruct Esteban, hopes to keep him out of trouble. In a setting with limited resources, folks like J-nathan, the teachers at the Rock school, and Jenny and Aben do a heroic job without public accolades. It reminds me the words of the apostle Paul in 1 Corinthians 13:1: "If I speak in the tongues of men or of angels, but do not have love, I am only a resounding gong or a clanging cymbal."

Oscar, an eleven-year-old boy, recently moved back to the mountains after his father, with whom he had been living, was jailed. Our church and medical team searched for Oscar on a hot afternoon, only to have his mother inform us that Oscar was spending the afternoon with his aunt. We were disappointed because we wanted to find out whether Oscar was suffering from depression due to the many losses he had experienced.

We decided to talk to his mother in her small shack built into the mountain. Oscar had moved back in with her a year earlier, enrolling in the public school. She said he had developed a thick cataract in his right eye as a two-year-old and the doctors she sought told her there was no cure. She seemed hesitant and unclear about his diagnosis. Taken aback by our concern for Oscar and the gifts we had brought for him, she was even more shocked that we wanted to care for her health by doing a blood pressure check. She gratefully accepted our offer to pray for her needs and gladly asked Jesus to enter her heart. She agreed to visit our church and clinic with Oscar the next day.

Oscar stepped into the wooden, student desk chair, which functioned as my medical office, guided by his mother. Questions arose in my mind. Could Oscar see enough to read? Did he feel alone back in this mountain community? Was he able to make friends? How did he do in school? Was he depressed, as one would assume? Did he miss his father? Surprised by his boyish young voice that pointed to the young side of eleven years, I found Oscar approachable but serious. He told me he had a friend named David, a neighbor whom he had befriended during their brief childhood in Los Pinos. The friendship was renewed with Oscar's return.

Oscar liked school, particularly studying and drawing. When asked, he read the front cover of the children's Bible we gave him, but became angry when asked to read the small print of Genesis. Backing off, we told Oscar the story of God's creation, explaining that trees and animals, including my black Labrador Retriever guide dog, "Paros," at my feet were created by God. Oscar petted Paros at my invitation.

"Hey, Oscar how do you know for sure that God made trees? Does the Bible in front of you say so?" I asked.

"Yes," Oscar replied, pointing to the word "arboles." How about dogs? Oscar said the word, "perro," wasn't in the book but he felt that dogs were also created by God. Clearly, Oscar could see. So this young man could read and enjoy studying as he claimed.

"Oscar, could you read more?" Anger rose again. So we gave Oscar paper and crayons to draw, while we focused on speaking with his mother. "He'll draw cars," she said. "That's what he likes best."

After ten to fifteen minutes of conversation with mom, I anxiously asked to know what Oscar had drawn. I wondered: Was it a car? Was it a sad depiction of some lonely child with head hung down? Was it a dark scene from his mind? Many times pictures from children are a great reflection of their mood or state of mind.

Amazingly, Oscar began with a beautiful sunflower in the center of the paper. He embellished the scene with bright clouds and the mountains of his home. Brilliant and colorful, this remarkable drawing, centered perfectly on the paper, did not reflect a sullen mood but a hopeful, optimistic child, resilient in the midst of hardship.

How long will it remain that way for Oscar? I wondered.

If the Rock church and God have any input, hopefully it will be forever, for on that day, Oscar placed his trust in Jesus Christ as his Lord and Savior.

I gently held the beautiful drawing Oscar gave me and placed it in my bag to frame and cherish when I returned to my home in New York.

Questions for personal consideration and/or group discussion:

1. What is your initial reaction to this chapter?

2. Were you aware that this situation exists—hundreds of young children trying to cross into the U.S. due to their squalid, apparently unchangeable conditions? If so, have you tried to do something about it?

3. José, Esteban, and Oscar are children whose lives crossed Dr. Eng's, by God's grace. Each of them had unique stories, as do we all. Review each case description and describe how you might try to help one of these boys.

4. When you read that six-foot-tall "Jenny" relocated to Honduras several years ago to try to help, what is your response:

    a. Wow, that takes a lot of commitment.

    b. I'm glad there are people like Jenny still in our world today.

    c. I think I would like to help her, if I could find a way.

    d. All of the above.

5. As you read Oscar's story, how did you relate to Dr. Eng and her team trying to find him, to see if he might be suffering from depression due to the many losses he had experienced?

    a. I wondered what kind of difference they thought they could make?

b. I was glad they found him and were able to help him, including his spiritual needs.

c. I learned a little more about resolve in action.

6. It inspired me to think about what kind of difference I can make in the life of even one person who crosses my path.

Just as a body, though one, has many parts, but all its many parts form one body, so it is with Christ. Now you are the body of Christ, and each one of you is a part of it.

1 Corinthians 12:12, 27

Chapter 7

The Parable of Paros

My name is Paros. I am a black Labrador Retriever. I am a guide dog, taking my mommy wherever she tells me to go. Even though she's my "mommy," other people like to call her Elaine, and some others call her "Doctor." To me she is "mommy."

I want to tell you what happened yesterday when mommy took me to a meeting where there were a bunch of two-legged persons also called "doctors." I think they were talking about how to help God out with something called CMDA or something like that. I'm not good with letters or words like my mommy and her friends: Aunt Meredith, Uncle Randy, Aunt Jennifer, Uncle Matthew, Uncle David, and Aunt Karis. There were also two other ladies, I think one of them was called Deanne. She was trying to help the CMDA in my city figure out what they were supposed to do. They spent a lot of time trying to figure out who they were.

That seemed strange to me. Don't they already know? I know I am a dog. I look like a dog. I behave like a dog. I eat kibble like a dog. And I don't know why I should find the right words to say what I am. I think it took them a "kibbillion minutes" to come up with ten words to tell everybody what CMDA in our city was.

They would have kept going if that nice lady Deanne didn't stop them because they were out of time. They finally came up with, "Strengthening Christian Doctors and Dentists to Fulfill Their God-given Calling." *Ok, OK that's very nice,* I thought, *but can't we get on to important things . . . like that yummy looking brown thing on Uncle David's plate?* I think they call it a "chocolate" muffin. It's made of the stuff mommy never keeps in the house because she says it's poisonous for dogs. But I think Dad sneaks some into his room. I get a taste of it whenever he drops one of those colorful ovals, with chocolate covering a peanut, and the letters M and M on it. It never bothered me before.

Well, I had to have some excitement while they were all talking so when Uncle David wasn't looking I grabbed the chocolate muffin. Wow, that was the biggest kibble I ever had! I gobbled it up real quick before my mommy got to me. I surprised them at how fast I could put it down—less than two seconds! The group went on to talk and talk more and more about those ten words and how they want to strengthen people to do God's work.

My mommy told me about God. She and I tell Jesus, each night, "Thank you for bringing us together." She asks Jesus to protect me wherever she brings me places like Thailand and Cuba. Then she's says "Amen," and I know I can go to sleep. I try not to snore before she says "Amen" because that would not be nice to God. He protects us while we sleep.

It's real simple. I don't know why it is so hard for people to ask God to help them do things. I don't know why they spend so much time with words. If mommy says just one word like, "Sit," I sit." If she says, "Paros, forward," I walk straight ahead. I bet if God told those doctors to do what he wants them to do, they would do it. But, it looks like they have to write it down with just the right words and make the right plans. Oh well. What do I know, I am just a dog? My mommy says we dogs "live in the moment," whatever that means.

I love my mommy's friends, but they were beginning to really bore me with words. Blah, blah, blah. Why can't she take out my toys from her bag? I know she put them there. I can smell my ball and my "tug o' war" rope.

Then things got really interesting. Lunch! Aunt Karis told mom there were "wraps" with chicken and other stuff in them. Uncle David said that there were salads with something called fruit that his wife Aunt Janet made. Thanks Uncle David for the chocolate muffin but I think I'll pass on the fruit. Everybody got up to get food, so I thought, *Here's my chance.* I sneaked out to the room where all the aunties do "peepee and poopoo" because I remember seeing a lot of my favorite snacks in a nice big bowl on the bathroom floor . . . paper towels. I love them. They're so yummy . . . nice and chewy, smells so appetizing, sometimes they come loaded with gravy especially at McDonald's. Others that I find in the park come smeared with sweat, like Gatorade in a soft taco! So while all those doctors weren't looking I ate and stuffed as many towels as I could into my mouth, and my tummy was so full! And they still couldn't find me.

I heard my mommy call, "Come, Paros." I'm supposed to answer her right away, because "Come" is a word that means hurry. But I couldn't help it. The towels were too good. I love my

> **I don't know why it is so hard for people to ask God to help them do things. If mommy says just one word like, "Sit," I sit. If she says, "Paros, forward," I walk straight ahead.**

mommy and her friends because they all want very much to help people who are sick and to help them come to know Jesus. And now they are meeting all day trying to figure how to strengthen doctors and dentists to do this. Words don't seem to work for me. I just believe in doing. Doing gets the job done and words just puts blotches on paper. I'd rather put the paper to good use and eat it, with a little sauce added!

Then I got into trouble. Uncle David found me and brought me back to the meeting. Mommy was mad at me for not listening to her and tied my leash to her chair. I was now listening to more words like "Who is our target?" and "What do they value?" It was my punishment. So many words are not good for a dog's ears, but all those two-legged doctors loved it. Then suddenly my tummy began to really hurt. Arggh . . . Baarf . . . I threw up brown stuff. They were shocked as it landed on what they call "linoleum" and relieved that it had not hit the "carpet." But then I got the carpet, too!

Aunt Meredith quickly came over to check on me and said she would take me outside to get fresh air. Uncle Randy and Uncle David came over to see what I threw up. They told my mommy it was brown-colored, and began to clean up the stuff with a big box of paper with alcohol and a vacuum cleaner. I could have told them that it was the big chocolate kibble I had taken from Uncle David's plate. I wanted to eat it up again but they wouldn't let me. Shucks. Oh, oh. My tummy became a volcano again and out came my paper snacks. Oh no. Oh no. Aunt Jennifer sprang to action. "I'm going to get gloves for us all, remember I'm an infectious disease specialist," she said. I don't know what she meant by that. She looked pretty healthy to me.

But she was so helpful, I didn't let her words bother me. In fact, everybody was doing things to help. Uncle Matthew had taken me out to pee earlier, so Mommy could concentrate on the meeting. Aunt Karis kept clearing mommy's dishes from the table and then guided her around when I was too sick to do my job. Uncle Randy kept checking if I was alright. I kept throwing up and was too sick to do anything but watch all my auntie and uncle doctors go into action taking care of me, cleaning up all afternoon. They worked like a body, just like how God said in the Bible: "Now you are the body of Christ, and each one of you is a part of it" (1 Corinthians 12:27).

My mommy felt bad because she wished she could do more. And she felt bad that I kept interrupting their meeting of making words and plans every time I vomited. I wanted to keep the paper inside of me but my belly wouldn't let it. I hoped Uncle Randy wouldn't have to go inside me and take it out of my tummy. I had heard that he is a surgeon.

I also felt bad that that nice lady Deanne was trying to help everyone but everyone was trying to help me. I wonder if they saw what I was seeing. They were doing what I have been saying from the beginning. Actions or doing is much better than words. When they were running around helping each other help me and my mommy, weren't they doing what they said CMDA was supposed to do: "Strengthening Christian doctors and dentists to fulfill their God-given calling?"

All those things they did at that meeting helped me and mommy do her "doctor calling." She's blind and if her doctor friends and I didn't help her she would never be able to do the things God has called her to do. God was right when he said Christians work like a body so that together it works well. I know. I have four paws, two floppy ears, a very keen nose, and a "big mouth for food and paper." All these parts work well together to make me a good dog. Jesus will make CMDA in New York work like a body just like mine, just like all the Christian doctor aunties and uncles in that meeting, and that will make CMDA continue to help strengthen more Christian doctors and dentists to fulfill their God-given calling around the world.

"Just as a body, though one, has many parts, but all its many parts form one body, so it is with Christ" (1 Corinthians 12:12).

Questions for personal consideration and/or group discussion:

1. What did you think of the dog's perspective on a group of doctors taking a "kibbillion" minutes to come up with ten words to describe their ministry?

2. The dog lives in the present. When "mommy" says "sit," the dog sits; when mommy says "forward," the dog goes forward. So why is it so hard for humans to have the same response to the will of God, when they know it?

3. Paros likes to snack on paper towels with sticky or stinky stuff on them. By analogy (parable), are humans this way sometimes. If so, what results are common?

4. The dog even wanted to eat it again. Does that remind you of anyone?

5. In the end, the group functioned as a body, each doing its own part to deal with the situation and move beyond it. The dog knew this. Do you think the doctors did? If so, what lesson might they have learned from this near-catastrophe?

Praise be to the God and Father of our Lord Jesus Christ, the Father of compassion and the God of all comfort, who comforts us in all our troubles, so that we can comfort those in any trouble with the comfort we ourselves receive from God.

2 Corinthians 1:3-4

Chapter 8

A Life Worth Living

Two and a half years ago, Dr. James Avery, at that time the medical director of the Visiting Nurse Service Hospice Program, offered me the opportunity to study the discipline of hospice and palliative medicine under his sponsorship. I had told him how much I admired this specialty because it offered an opportunity to integrate medicine and spiritual care in a holistic way that far exceeded what my own career in psychiatry had done. This opportunity was time limited as the boards would only be offered on November 16, 2010, and a last time in 2012 for board certified practitioners like myself. Otherwise we would have to retrain in a fellowship program. Thus followed a period of intense study and experiences with terminal patients at Calvary Hospital and over 100 team hours with the interdisciplinary team of doctors, social workers, chaplains, and nurses with the VNS Home hospice program.

The terminal phase of a person's life offers a unique opportunity to address one's life narrative. This is a time one hopes for strengthening relationship bonds and creating legacies with family and mending broken bridges. Patients and their families may recall life's highlights with photos, writings, memorabilia, and intimate conversation. These are woven into one's life tapestry. Finding meaning with God, conveying and receiving forgiveness, and a vision of the afterlife are important spiritual tasks at this time. All this is done while doctors and nurses attend carefully to the comfort needs of those suffering painful and destructive illnesses, seeking the optimal, albeit limited, quality of life the patients deserve. Simultaneously the treating team must address many of the emotional and burdensome needs of the caregivers. "Is this life worth living?" is a question often posed as the tasks of dying are performed. To my observation, the answer has always been yes; this was a life worth living.

As an accommodation for my blindness, a reader was to be provided for me during the two day boards beginning November 16, 2010. This would take place at a testing center in Rego Park, N.Y. My husband had been praying for my grueling studies in which I had listened to nine books and reviewed all my notes using the voice software in my computer. But on those last three days he was moved to pray for, "My protection for seventy-two hours." Since I was entering new situations, he did not know what I would face. Ephesians 6:12 says, "For our struggle is not against flesh and blood, but against the rulers, against the authorities, against the powers of this dark world and against the spiritual forces of evil in the heavenly realms."

My mentor, Mary, had called to pray for me, mentioning that I needed to "Count my blessings" and to "Comfort others with the comfort God gives." Honestly, my head was so crammed with medical facts for the boards that I couldn't ponder the implications of these prayers until much later. I thanked God for these and many other intercessors, but could not wait to spill out the details of my study onto the test. I was also burdened by a request by several people the week before to testify at a New York City Council meeting designed to pass legislation seeking to limit, if not destroy, the work of crisis pregnancy centers in New York. But I could not help these Christians in the pregnancy ministries, as it was the same day as my boards.

And then a wrench was thrown into the wheel. An e-mail arrived the day before the exam that the boards were cancelled due to a water main break outside the testing center and that despite all efforts they could not register me in the other test site in New York. To add to my turmoil, multiple phone calls to the American Board of Internal Medicine, and to the main headquarters of the testing center yielded nothing but tedious voicemail menus. By noon that day, despite having to see patients at various time slots, I knew that if I did not cry, I would explode and so I filled up tissues all over my desk. I did not care anymore how bad my face or makeup looked. One of my afternoon patients commented, Dr. Eng, did you know you have two boxes of tissues on your desk? Your patients must be doing a lot of crying." I responded with a weak "Yeah. . . ."

Finally, I started receiving answers from the many panicked voice messages I had left and the callers all explained how virtually impossible it was to reschedule the test for many reasons, but especially because I needed an accommodations room. I told them I would be willing to fly out that night and go anywhere in the country not knowing really if it could be done. They also told me that if they could not find anything before December 3, I would not be able to take it at all.

Then D.B. called from her hotel room, having been informed how upset I was by the American Board of Internal Medicine. I reiterated the difficulties, "D., I now know how hard it is for you to provide a test center and you know how hard it would be for me after two and a half years of study. Please do whatever you can and I will pray for you."

I proceeded to study some more in the next hour I had free. Right after my review of the last set of notes, D. called and told me after searching the entire northeast corridor, she had found a test site in Norwalk, Connecticut, which could give me the palliative medicine exam the following week. "I'll take it!" I called 411 to find the name of the only contacts I knew in Connecticut —a couple that had been in my church seven years earlier. I pleaded with the operator to check Darien . . . no result, maybe Stamford . . . no result. "How about New Canaan?"

"Yes there was one J.L. there."

Dialing the number, I must have sounded like a lunatic when the woman's voice answered. After she finally realized who I was and she listened to my story in rapid fire, the first thing she said was "This is of God. I know the building where you will be tested; it's right near me. I'll come get you after your last patient next week and bring you to my home and get you to the test site the next two days. And thank you for including me in this God-given plan." Wow. The amazing power of God and his awesome orchestrations energized me. Sovereign and mighty God, you have done the impossible.

With this comfort in my troubles, my thoughts turned to the New York City council hearing the next day. Now I only had about an hour to find out the details about the hearing location and book "My Access a Ride." (This is a vehicle that provides transportation for the disabled.) Suddenly I realized that I was totally unprepared for this hearing. Plus, I'm really a gentle soul and find it hard to address opinionated politicians, radical feminists and the argumentative powers that rule the abortion industry. But after what God had done for me in his strength, what could mortal man do to me?

The next day, my driver ushered me into the building at 250 Broadway to a security desk, bypassing a large mob of people prepared to do battle for either the pro-life or pro-choice front. Being blind, I received some attention and a guard brought me upstairs to the hearing room and asked where I wanted to sit.

"Right next to the microphone," I said and so he led me there to a seat in the front row. I also asked to sign the Sergeant at Arms list in order to speak. I sat down realizing I knew so little about the case and prayed that the Lord would not make me go first. He answered that prayer exceedingly well as I sat there alone from 12:00 noon to about 7:00 pm, when I finally got to give my testimony.

In the hours of waiting, my questions about the case were being answered by overhearing the conversations of the strangers pouring into the room, then seated around me. Each time I had a logistical question someone would ask the same question to a neighbor and I would receive my answer ("Holy Eavesdropping"). When the proceeding started, the heated arguments on both sides brought more clarity about the issues and by 5 pm I had a twenty minutes' testimony in my head. However, over the next two hours the time limit to speak was cut down to two minutes per person. In order to control the time, the court administrator kept hitting the "time's up" bell simultaneously yelling "Thank you, thank you." Her words would get louder and more threatening if a speaker passed the two-minute deadline.

Now how could I turn my twenty minute's talk to two minutes? By this time, it was clear to my totally wasted and inept brain that the only way I could make any sense or have any effect was by the power of the Holy Spirit to give me the words. So when I gingerly made my way to the speakers' microphone with my white cane, the Lord gave me these words to say:

> My name is Dr. Elaine Eng and I started out in medicine as an obstetrician-gynecologist, but because of illness retrained in psychiatry where I have practiced for twenty years. And now I'm embarking on a board specialty of hospice and palliative medicine. It is an "act of God" that I am here as I am supposed to be taking my board exam today but a water main broke at the test site causing them to cancel my test. You have heard the testimonies of the many good things done by crisis pregnancy centers in New York and I am here as an educator, participant, and at times in leadership, and can testify to the good done.
>
> I have also seen the good replicated throughout the country in Spokane, Washington, California, Colorado, and Florida where I have had a chance to teach and meet others in the field. Beyond this I have had the privilege to participate in the good replicated around the world first in the Crisis Pregnancy Center of Kenya, under the auspices of Grace Ojiambo. Confronting the scourge of AIDS, I traveled to the crisis pregnancy center in southern Taiwan. This center, under the leadership of the Bedwells helped many young women with their sexual health concerns. In Tokyo I met the pregnancy ministry leader who brought a little baby from his birth mother to the loving arms of his adoptive parents. Never in my experiences have I seen the malicious or deceptive practices you have accused crisis centers of doing. (That was the first minute.)
>
> But on a more personal note, in 1953 a poor Chinese woman immigrated to this country and was pregnant with daughter #1. She and her husband were trying to eke out a meager living in this city. In 1958 she conceived daughter #3. If this couple had been transported to this

millennium, genetic tests would soon be developed to show that both daughters had the genes that would lead to incurable blindness. I would sure hope that there would be a crisis pregnancy center counseling them on the alternatives to abortion. For if not, there would be one less woman in the graduating class of Princeton University in 1976, one less physician graduating from the Albert Einstein College of Medicine in 1980. My husband would not have had a wife and my two grown children would never have been conceived.

Ding, the bell rang. And there was an unusual pause for a long time. I did not know what to do as I couldn't see. When the court administrator finally recovered her voice, she thanked me. The case was wrapped up after a couple more speakers and I got up to find a cab to go home. However, as I tried to exit the hearing room, I was stopped by several people.

C.S., the head of twelve crisis pregnancy centers in New York came up and told me how powerful my testimony was and he said that he and many others wanted to get up and give me a standing ovation, but they were prohibited from doing so. The head of Care Net Pregnancy Centers introduced herself and thanked me. A lawyer from the American Center for Law and Justice came up to thank me for my strengthening testimony and I was able to thank her for the legal work she had done to help Christians in matters like this. I had just heard her voice on radio the day before. And finally an unknown woman just came up and grabbed me and kissed me.

What had the Lord accomplished? He told the audience, that mine and not just mine but all are lives are worth living. There is no God-given life that needs to be aborted or euthanized. But he was able to say it in an unusual and effective way. My brain could not process or understand all of the events that had happened, but my soul turned its attention to the prayers of some of my intercessors in those thirty-six hours. He answered the prayer for protection uttered by my husband, as he protected me from the fierce fighting and argumentation I so loathe. My mentor's prayers were also granted in that God wanted me to count my blessings and it was framed uniquely in the testimony to the NYC council. Psalm 103:2 says, "Praise the Lord, my soul, and forget not all his benefits." Finally the verse on how I needed to comfort others with the compassion he has given me was fulfilled in the opportunity to strengthen the many people in the good work done in pregnancy centers sharing the gospel of Christ in word and deed.

Many years ago a young teenager became pregnant out of wedlock. She would carry a child who would only live thirty-three years. Would we ever contest that that was not a life worth living? As the Son of God, Jesus did what no man could do, enter earth because of his great love for mankind, die a humiliating death on a brutal, wooden cross, so that those who would trust and believe in him as Lord and Savior would have a restored relationship with the God who so much wants to adopt us as his sons and daughters. In order to make us holy like him, he had to pay the consequences of our sin and brokenness. He then triumphantly rose from the grave to prove that he is King of Kings and Lord of Lords. It is this Jesus who is the very source of my blessings, my protection, and my comfort. May he be yours as well.

Questions for personal consideration and/or group discussion:

1. Providing care during the last phase of a patient's life can be challenging and enervating. Workers in this field sometimes wonder: "Is this life worth living?" as they perform their tasks for the dying. Why might someone feel this way?

2. If you were a caretaker in a Hospice setting, which of the following would you seek to practice:

   ___ To look for the positive in each case, and to try to help families retain their hope.

   ___ To try to comfort families by remaining cheerful and alert to their needs.

   ___ To never stop caring about everyone affected.

3. The author's prayer supporter suggested that she try to "comfort others with the comfort God gives." How can this happen in an end-of-life situation?

4. How do you think that the author's experience of being a "wanted" vs. an "inconvenient" child has affected her tenacity and resolve?

5. Imagine yourself giving testimony in the court case she describes. With only two minutes to introduce the light of truth into a very dark setting, how would you proceed?

> *Then they cried out to the LORD in their trouble, and he brought them out of their distress. He stilled the storm to a whisper; the waves of the sea were hushed. They were glad when it grew calm, and he guided them to their desired haven.*
>
> Psalm 107:28-30.

Chapter 9

A Call Worth Pursuing

On October 29, 2012, Hurricane Sandy struck New York City with vehemence. My husband and I sat at the dinner table celebrating my guide dog's third birthday, apprehensive about the roaring winds and the dangling limbs of our neighbor's tree in the back of our house. It had been a turbulent year marked by surgery for a possible malignancy, which thankfully yielded a benign diagnosis. I had transitioned to a new job as a full-time professor in counseling, and a call from God led to a determined effort to study for the boards in hospice and palliative medicine. Why would a wise and rational God ask a blind woman, graced with a twenty-three-year career in psychiatry, and a fulfilling role as a teacher, to pursue a new vocation in hospice? Still, whenever the Lord calls, one cannot rest unless one obeys even if nothing about the call makes sense nor is there any guarantee that it was building up to a known goal.

My journey had begun in 2008 when Dr. Jim Avery started me on the program that would lead to certification in this specialty if I were to pass the boards. A big impasse dampened my resolve when I failed the boards in 2010 by nine points. Thinking I had misread God's call, I gladly decided not to consider retaking the boards offered to me one final time in 2012. But, when the still small voice and circumstance spoke God's call again, I reapplied to take the boards.

I wondered: *How can I study for this specialty when blindness makes information so much less available?* The Lord put me in the path of Ms. Weir and Julie Bruno at the American Academy of Hospice and Palliative medicine. Julie was an administrator for the review course offered by the academy for board preparation. She took a keen interest in trying to understand what would help me learn. The books and CDs I had tried to use previously were ineffective in providing all the information I needed in a coherent form, as the technology for scanning or downloading information did not mesh with my talking computer. Julie and I had several discussions over numerous weeks of research and discovered the best way for me to learn was to create mp3s of all the lectures related to the course and I would learn by listening over and over again to all the files. I have always claimed that "repetition is the mother of learning" to my students and listening to the same voices speaking on pain management, family counseling, depression, and spiritual care pounded the needed material into my brain over the months.

Well, I guess I'm as ready as I will be, I told myself and God in October with the exam scheduled for November 13. Then Sandy hit at 6 pm, a thunderous crack struck the driveway and the side of our house followed by seismic boom to our roof. A one-hundred-year-old sycamore tree impaled itself into our attic, taking down live wires with it. Both our side and back entrances were blocked by massive limbs and our front door was curtained by sparkling live wires. Even if we were to escape through the front with Paros our guide dog, the hurricane force winds would have blown us into unknown dangers. We were in peril going out and potential peril staying in. That night Paros and I huddled near the front door, trying to sleep, but ready to bolt out into danger should our home ignite or crumble. With the winds still whipping the impaled tree in our house like an egg beater, I asked the Lord to keep us safe. The next day a building inspector slapped a summons on our front door stating that our home was uninhabitable until a licensed professional evaluated it. With just two weeks before the boards, Paros and I were nomads traveling from home to home of friends who generously took us in.

It wasn't easy, but Paros, our ever-steady black Labrador Retriever took to the changes with grace and aplomb, guiding me ever so faithfully in new terrain. With this stress, I knew that I would pass the boards only with the Lord's miraculous intervention. There was so much going against a comfortable approach to the exam. The day came and Paros and I were circling around, lost in the gardens exiting where we had been staying. We finally arrived at the test center, very stressed as we met the reader who recorded and assisted me with the exam over two days.

When it was over, I received a call from our architect friend, that the house was approved for living. Paros and I returned to a cold, very damaged, but familiar home. On December 24, 2012, I receive my very first Christmas present, a letter congratulating me on passing the hospice and palliative medicine exam for Board certification. God

> With the winds still whipping the impaled tree in our house like an egg beater, I asked the Lord to keep us safe.

faithfully accomplished his plan for me.

On Feb. 2013, I met with Dr. Jarry Richardson at the Christian Medical and Dental Association's Education conference in Thailand. "What do I do with this board certification," I asked him? And in missionary counseling, has anyone paid special attention to the needs of terminally ill missionaries or their elderly loved ones and family members?

"No one that I can think of," he replied. "Why don't we begin to consider this?"

A light bulb went on in both of our heads. Member care has included attention to missionary children, marriages, singles on the field, but no mention of member care for the dying. Yet it is a critical need not anticipated by those serving the Lord. We agreed to work on it, and we hope to present this to "Mental Health and Missions" conferences, if given the opportunity.

So completes my understanding of God's call, a call worth pursuing.

Questions for personal consideration and/or group discussion:

1. The first time around, the author failed the boards in hospice and palliative medicine. Had this been your experience would you have:

    ___ become even more determined to pass it the next time?

    ___ become discouraged enough to give up what you had thought was God's plan?

    ___ wonder how a blind physician could possibly pass this board as well?

2. The author learned by listening to mp3s of all the lectures related to the course, over and over. How would you handle this approach?

   ___ I'm not primarily an auditory learner, but it's not a bad way to augment the printed materials that I can see, versus her limitations.

   ___ It seems prudent for me to add this method to my way of studying.

   ___ Without doubt, she was not willing to not succeed withthis. Perhaps we could say that perseverance is the mother of invention, but resolve is the fuel that drives the engine forward.

3. For a moment, imagine yourself huddling with your guide dog, Paros, near your front door while hurricane "Sandy" pounded your neighborhood, and in particular your own home. Now add to this stress the stress of having to take the exam over the next two days. How would you do? What would you do? How would you keep a quiet mind in the midst of so much noise?

4. The long-term result of all this effort may be the development of a new focus for medical missionaries on end-of-life issues. "Member care for the dying" is the way the author describes this vision. Now, using your God-given imagination, think of how you might be able to become involved in such a focus.

If you say, "The LORD is my refuge," and you make the Most High your dwelling, no harm will overtake you, no disaster will come near your tent. For he will command his angels concerning you to guard you in all your ways; they will lift you up in their hands, so that you will not strike your foot against a stone. "Because he loves me," says the LORD, "I will rescue him; I will protect him, for he acknowledges my name. He will call on me, and I will answer him; I will be with him in trouble, I will deliver him and honor him. With long life I will satisfy him and show him my salvation."

PSALM 91:9-16

Chapter 10

Faith Vision

"Spirit of the Living God, fall afresh on me." [5]

On March 22, 2016, the Lord designed an epilogue to my life when an SUV struck me as I was crossing the street with my guide dog. Four days earlier, I had had an unusual dream where I saw in living color, a red pool of blood, shaded in beautiful coral. Two ministering angels were marveling at its brightness, while a gray shadow lay prone in the background. One of the angels moaned, "Oh no," but she clearly was not troubled, just tranquilly pensive. The other was smiling calmly. Both were glowing in golden lights. I felt awed with an amazing peace in my dream as I gazed at the radiant angels and marveled with them at the splotch of richly colored blood.

The next day my professor, Dr. Ronald Walborn was teaching a lesson on "pneumatology," the study of the Holy Spirit. Reading the text from John 20, just like the disciples, he invited us to request more of the work of the Holy Spirit in our lives. As we entered into a time of worship and prayer, I literally saw a vision of

> I had had an unusual dream where I saw in living color a red pool of blood, shaded in beautiful coral. Two ministering angels were marveling at its brigtness, while a gray shadow lay prone in the background.

my deceased earthly father, whose salvation had been a mystery to me. He had died suddenly more than a decade previously without making it known to us whether he had asked Christ into his life. I recognize the oddity of my statement, that a blind person could see so clearly in dreams and now, while conscious, see a vision in living color detailing facial features, distinctive garb, and the smiling demeanor of a parent. But this is what happened, whether explicable supernaturally or not.

If one has never been in an accident, it is difficult to completely understand the experience. Without eyesight, the event is beyond capture. At first I did not even know what had happened. *Did I walk into a wall? Why couldn't I get across the street?* Then, moments later, *Why am I lying flat on my back?* Conscious, I relied on my hearing to paint the picture of the event. The screams of the passers-by revealed to me that I had been struck by a vehicle.

"Call an ambulance!"

"Don't move her!"

These comments alerted me that my condition was serious and that I must have been left in the middle of the pedestrian grid. My first thought went to Paros.

"Someone get my dog," I yelled, not being able to move.

"We've got her," a woman's voice replied.

"Is she alright?" I asked. "Yes," she reassured me.

The next moments were a flurry of questions and activities as I was worked on by the paramedics and loaded into the ambulance. My husband was awakened by the frantic call that I had been hit by a car and that he should come quickly to pick up Paros.

In the ambulance, not knowing what would become of my time on earth, I remained remarkably calm as I recalled the vision of my father, and sensed that I would have at least one of my biological relatives in my heavenly home, a destination that I was rapidly but peacefully approaching.

> *I will give thanks to you, for I am fearfully and wonderfully made; Wonderful are Your works, and my soul knows it very well* (Psalm 139:14, NASB).

My physical health had been preserved by a keen interest in nutrition, medicine, and God's provision of relatively good health except for the diagnosis of retinitis pigmentosa at the age of twenty-nine that would lead to blindness. Because of this disability, I had spent the next thirty plus years developing coping skills, new learning techniques, and marveling at the faithfulness of God to allow me to make progress in my psychiatric career, role as mother and wife, a full-time professor at Nyack, and now a seminary student.

In 2015, while teaching a class on self-care, I had come upon a lesson on Personal Wellness Planning in which the question about my own self-care was posed to me for the first time in my life. Challenged to look at this area of weakness, it became clear that rest was suboptimal due to my schedule of night classes and ministry obligations. Setting the date for improvement, I had increased the hours for sleep and set limits on unnecessary evening activities for this past year.

However, nothing shocks a person to focus on physical wellness like being hit by an SUV. Listening as the paramedics and the trauma unit in the emergency room worked on me—listing each area of injury, addressing all vital organs that might have sustained damage, and being run through scans immediately for the brain, pelvis, abdomen, and skeleton—provided me with a personal anatomy lesson reminder. Needless to say, the presence of God and his angels at the accident spared my life and gave me every opportunity to observe myself.

Shock and denial kept tempting me to think, *I don't think I need an ambulance* (which I did not say). Nor did I tell the doctor, "I really did not need sutures, couldn't you just put a butterfly band aid over it?" I did tell the attending physician that I did not want an abdominal CT scan as it would give me too much radiation exposure. I realized how foolish all my expressions of denial were and gave in to all treatments and evaluations, which in retrospect were highly necessary. But the endorphin levels that the Lord designed in the body after trauma were such an anesthetic balm. So I did not feel most of my injuries initially, but they manifested in pain over the next several hours and days. If the doctor did not describe my multiple injuries, I would not have known them all until the swelling and pain appeared. Of course, being blind contributed to this peculiarity.

I recuperated by creating new self-care goals, which included adequate rest to allow for healing, nutrition focused on replacing iron from blood loss, giving myself permission to receive more aid from others, and grace not to push myself to accomplish the many demands on my life. All this is difficult for an over-achieving, neurotic Asian doctor, but my family friends and bosses helped to keep me accountable to this intention. I also needed to attend to the welfare of my guide dog, as we are a team, so the guide dog school would be supervising us on how to work together after a vehicular trauma. Thankfully the dog escaped being hit, another work of grace.

During the early days of my recuperation, I suspended all thought of my planned trip to work with the missionaries in

Greece. Racked with pain, how could I even get out of bed to board a plane and make any meaningful contribution to Kingdom work? Yet each day, the painful wounds slowly resolved. First there was the facial swelling, which made me look like Sylvester Stallone portraying Rocky after his first fight. The scabs fell off one by one, starting with the smaller ones and progressing to the deeper wounds. The sutures were removed from my forehead five days later. My ribs, hips, and foot took longer to permit me to move without pain. In the middle of a restless night, I recalled my pre-accident dream and realized that the shadow on the ground next to the splotch of bright red blood was *me*.

This remembrance comforted me greatly as the Lord showed me that he knew what would happen and that he had sent angels to attend to me before, during, and after the accident. I am grateful that he had not shown me that I was the shadow before, as that would have been too much information (TMI), and too overwhelming for me. But the tranquil, transcendent aura of the dream heralded God's superintention of the event.

Eighteen days later, I boarded a plane to Athens, completely healed and pain free. I landed in Greece with tears of gratitude for this miraculous and complete recovery in such a short time, ready to serve him among the missionaries convening on the Aegean coast.

Why did God allow me to go? Counseling, teaching, and supporting missionaries is his vocation for my life. Their valuable contribution to his kingdom work invites me to be like those who upheld Moses' arms as he led God's chosen people. After doing this for fifteen years, I now have the privilege to teach how to care for missionaries—educating students at Alliance Graduate School of Counseling and Alliance Theological Seminary at Nyack College. Casting a vision for supporting missionaries, also called "member care," with our training is so rewarding. As a full-time professor, it gives me great joy to design global service learning (GSL) classes and bring students to places such as Cuba, Thailand, Honduras,

Kenya, and Europe. Each class of students derives life-changing benefit as they learn how to come alongside those who devote themselves to ministry and mission. Some are even led to prayerfully consider a lifetime career of missionary work as counselors.

Kenya, the destination of eleven students and me, gave ample opportunity for learning at the Tumaini Counseling Center and Africa International University (formerly the Nairobi Evangelical Graduate School of Theology). Our students bonded with African students, sharing their life narratives with each other as they learned from professors at the school. They formed relationships that rival the best that could be formed in the United Nations. Some staff commented that they have never experienced outsiders who paid such great attention to their personal lives. Much of this was accomplished by ethnographic interviewing, supervened by God's love, and sanctified mutual respect.

Service and ministry opportunities were afforded by visits to the orphanage supported by a former Alliance professor, Dr. Eve Tolley. Our hearts were touched by the wonderful Kenyan children who were delightful in their playfulness, but inspirational in the manner in which they took care of each other and served us. It was so special that I had a hard time "peeling" my students away from playing with the children and finally had to threaten leaving them to find their way back to the campus with "motakari" (Swahili word for bus), local transport that would have been nearly impossible due to distance and overcrowding.

As a result of the tours of the Crisis Pregnancy Ministry of Kenya, the Tumaini counseling center, and photo opportunities with giraffes and other wildlife, the students felt they left their hearts in Africa. One actually returned to Kenya with her husband to serve in a Nairobi children's ministry.

Cuba, an impoverished but welcoming land, captured the attention of my next group of students. Walking into a lost land reminiscent of the 1950s of the U.S., we were alerted to the hunger of the people for Christ. The house church movement has experienced a great revival in this past decade and our students were surprised by how readily Cubans not only wanted to know the good news of Christ, but asked where they can go to worship him. We had never seen such receptiveness in our own country. We forged a strong relationship with local pastors as well as others we met at the seminary in Matansas.

In Paris, another GSL class experienced the opposite end of the spectrum, a place where the missionaries faced the lack of receptivity to Christ in a post-modern environment. So our group worked passionately at encouraging those missionaries who serve in the city working among the French people, immigrants to Paris from other countries, and sex-trafficked populations. Then we went on to do the same for those serving in Vienna. Many of the missionaries commented that they felt they were obligated to help our class learn, but instead they experienced unexpected support and counsel from our students. It seems the students experienced their first taste of member care without knowing it.

Thailand thrilled the tired group that traveled almost thirty hours to get there. Jet lag and fatigue did not stop them from settling down at a missionary guest house, "The Juniper Tree," and quickly getting to know Thai culture and the staff around the complex. From there they traveled to learn and meet folks at the Christian Medical and Dental Education conference. They also made daily forays into the night market, getting their share of Thai iced tea, body massages, and rides on the "tuk tuk" (Thai word for motorized rickshaw). The most meaningful part of this global service learning class was that one of my students applied to serve at the Cornerstone Counseling Center in Thailand upon graduation. This fulfilled my vision to teach students in order to pass along the legacy of using their degree in counseling to care for missionaries.

Returning to my home in May, I was regaled by a fragrance so delightfully intoxicating, I thought I had been transported to the island of Hawaii. My husband and friend, Mei, surprised me with a flowering plant from Taiwan that was planted for me specifically because I yearned to enjoy fragrances from God's creation. It is a blessing to survive a serious accident in order to experience this and my sixty-second birthday. So I made a note of earthly things the Lord wanted me to enjoy before my transport to my great eternal home.

Ecclesiastes states that it is a gift of God to be able to enjoy what you eat, what you drink, and the fruit of your labors (Ecclesiastes 3:12, 5:18-19). So on May 10, 2016, God gave me an encouraging nod when I received a reward from our school. My colleagues described the beautiful iridescent green glass plaque etched with "Faculty Commitment to Missions Award." My legacy is being noticed on earth, which means it is another crown that I will have to return and cast back to the Lord when I see him.

The third major blessing was being able to celebrate our fortieth wedding anniversary in Hawaii with my husband, Cliff, and our two grown children, Brian and Genevieve, who flew in to join us. And of course our ever faithful guide dog, Paros, traveled with us, nestled on a fleece blanket in the space in front of our feet. One of our Hawaiian friends, "Auntie May," says that when Paros retires, she will take her to the beach robed in a doggie hula skirt, bikini, and let her drink water in a champagne glass with a little blue umbrella.

Questions for personal consideration and/or group discussion:

1. Prior to her incident with the SUV, the author experienced what she takes to be a supernatural view of the event, in full color, with glowing angels, blood, and a grey shadow (herself) prone on the ground. How do you relate to this story?

___ This was a gift from God.

___ My theological background makes me wonder about the source and veracity of something like this.

___ I can accept this, even though I've never experienced anything like this, myself.

2. "At first I did not even know what had happened. *Did I walk into a wall? Why couldn't I get across the street?* Then, moments later, *Why am I lying flat on my back?* Conscious, I relied on my hearing to paint the picture of the event. The screams of the passers-by revealed to me that I had been struck by a vehicle."

    ___ What is your initial reaction to this report?

    ___ I found it interesting and heart-warming that her first thoughts were about Paros, and I was relieved that the dog survived the incident uninjured.

    ___ I wanted to punch out the SUV driver for this carelessness.

    ___ I felt: "This is not right! Godly people whose only goal is to help others should not experience such things."

3. "However, nothing shocks a person to focus on physical wellness like being hit by an SUV. Listening as the paramedics and the trauma unit in the emergency room worked on me —listing each area of injury, addressing all vital organs that might have sustained damage and being run through scans immediately for the brain, pelvis, abdomen, and skeleton— provided me with a personal anatomy lesson reminder."

    If you were in this situation, would you have reacted differently, the same, or unknown?

Knowing you were scheduled to present soon at an international conference, would you be:

___ Angry

___ Questioning whether that was still a good plan

___ Depressed that it was obviously impossible for me to fulfill that assignment.

___ Resolved that nothing could keep me from fulfilling God's will.

4. When you consider the text from this sentence on, what is your primary feeling:

"Eighteen days later, I boarded a plane to Athens, completely healed and pain free. I landed in Greece with tears of gratitude for this miraculous and complete recovery in such a short time, ready to serve him among the missionaries convening on the Aegean coast."

*For God so loved the world,
that he gave his only begotten Son,
that whosoever believeth in him
should not perish, but have
everlasting life.*

JOHN 3:16, KJV

Afterword

The Narrative of My Life

I became a Christian at age sixteen when a high school classmate brought me to her church. Located in Chinatown, NY, the altar had John 3:16 written in Chinese characters. "For God so loved the world that he gave his only begotten Son that whosoever believeth in him should not perish, but have everlasting life" (KJV).

The truth of this message touched my heart and it was not long before I asked Christ to be my Lord and Savior. God called me to the field of medicine (Ob-gyn), marriage, and two children. Then in 1983, I was diagnosed as having retinitis pigmentosa, an inherited eye disease that would lead to progressive blindness and in fact had already met the legal criteria for blindness. I was teaching the interns and junior residents how to deliver babies, which was routine for me, but I could not see clearly some of the things they were doing. I thought I just needed stronger glasses, but I found out it wasn't the case. Once I heard the diagnosis, I knew that I could not ethically practice in a surgical subspecialty. I resigned the next day.

Somehow I knew that God had made it possible to accept this news because I was now permitted to devote myself to full-time motherhood, a role that was important to me. You can imagine the surprise of my ophthalmologist when I accepted the news with peace of mind. Judging by the look on his face and the reaction of the Bellevue Ob-gyn department, this was a tragedy. But at that time I was in deep suffering from not being a mother to my two babies due to the long hours at the hospital. I had prayed for more than a year crying to God for a chance to be a full-time mother. The diagnosis of blindness was God's special answer to my prayer. I enjoyed years of full-time motherhood. It was a gift of God and I would not change my life in any other way. As Romans 8:28 says, God works all things for the good of those who love him (including things that are bad like blindness).

When my children started school I asked the Lord what he wanted to do with my career and life. Did he want me to pursue seminary training, or was there a career for me in medicine? My doctor told me that the only specialties I could practice were psychiatry or statistics research. I was not good in math so statistics was out. So with the advice and prayers of a Christian pediatrician, I returned to training in the field of psychiatry. The transition between the fields of Ob-gyn and psychiatry was quite dramatic. I had not even taken one psychology course in college and did not ever focus on psychiatry in medical school as that was not my intended area of study. Moreover, the anxiety I now faced in training as a blind physician became daunting. Learning an entirely new body of clinical information and adjusting to the intricacies and challenges of doing it blind would be difficult to say the least.

The department of psychiatry I applied to had preliminary discussions with other doctors in training as to whether they would want a disabled colleague. Most had hesitations and one was vehemently opposed. But the chairman, Dr. Vandersall, went to the administration and requested an extra position for me while the original vacancy was filled by a "normal" person. Hence I was the "extra help" rather than a burden who may not be able to hold her own. With this understanding, everyone agreed to take me on. Dr. Vandersall also encouraged me by telling me that as a person with a chronic illness, I could perhaps relate better to those whose mental health afflictions were also chronic, and vice versa.

During my years at the hospital, the faculty were interested and queried often as to how they could help me make progress. I felt comfortable in making suggestions tailored to what I was learning about my adaptive needs. Readers were hired. Office space was made handicap accessible. Some consultations were done with a partnering resident. He could read charts and I would do the evaluation. In the process, I realized that I was now the teacher to those around me as to what was best in the interest of my progress and adaptation.

I knew I had to be articulate while maintaining sensitivity to the concerns of my fellow residents and hospital staff. Professionally, as a psychiatric trainee, I became a keen observer, a student of the ranges of behaviors and reactions that others might have toward me. But personally, I did not want to be the entitled, demanding, helpless handicapped person. So the role of a teacher/collaborator with my colleagues allowed us to work successfully together. The team approach in the inpatient unit made it very congenial for this mindset and the nursing and ancillary staff were vital and gracious in supporting my work as a resident. I kept up my journal reading and read the standard psych texts already recorded in the Library of Congress. The Bible says "Faith is the substance of things hoped for, the evidence in things not seen" (Hebrews 11:1), and it was this faith in God that formed the conviction that I would succeed.

During my residency, objective tests showed that I had started at the bottom and by the time of graduation climbed to the top in terms of psychiatric knowledge. The process was clearly an achievement of a supportive environment, which I believe was orchestrated by God. Furthermore, I found that the wisdom in God's Word for counseling such as that found in Proverbs proved effective as I was learning the medical aspects. I've been blessed to pursue the integration of Scripture and medicine in my greater than twenty-five-year career in counseling, teaching, and writing.

Constance Pledger of the National Institute on Disability and Rehabilitation Research denotes a comprehensive paradigm for understanding disability. It promotes the concept that adaptation is influenced by the broader context of social, environmental, and individual factors. These play an important role in the sense of "disabled-ness" in our patients. It is painfully clear that we in the medical field cannot cure all illnesses or correct even the majority of impairments in our patients with chronic conditions. How then do we successfully help our patients adapt and gain mastery? We need to attend to the social, psychological, and spiritual factors that portend healing without actually curing the physical disease. Allied with the resources of an attentive medical team, a willing and flexible social environment, a person's mastery of chronic illness can occur.

I can only thank an almighty God for my own narrative and praise him for the special one that so many have. It is valuable to all brothers and sisters in the Lord. It will foster professional and kingdom bonds. The benefit, process, and facilitation of narrative sharing can be found in the book *The Transforming Power of Story: How Telling Your Story Brings Hope to Others and Healing to Yourself*. It is also taught and experienced in my courses at Nyack/Alliance Theological Seminary.

That book contains narratives of Christians whose life tragedies were redeemed by God for ministry or a greater good. They include healthcare workers, patients, missionaries, or people exposed to loss, illness, or life crises. The book also provides ways in which narrative venues ("Tell Your Story Forums") can be developed to benefit the church or community in order to strengthen the body of Christ.

To me the most important story that transforms is the Gospel of Jesus Christ.

~ Elaine Leong Eng, MD

Notes

1. Dekker, Jim "Resilience, Theology, and the Edification of Youth: Are We Missing a Perspective" (*Journal of Youth Ministry*, Spring 2011; Vol. 9, Issue 2).
2. Dekker, op cit, 68.
3. Biebel, David B. *If God is so Good, Why Do I Hurt So Bad?* (Arvada, CO, 2014: Healthy Life Press), 53. See www.healthylifepress.com, or Amazon.com to order.
4. Lyrics by Carolina Sandell (1865). In the public domain.
5. Lyrics by Daniel Iverson (1926). The hymn itself is copyright 1982, Hope Publishing Company; Carol Stream, IL 60188.

No Worries
Spiritual and Mental Health Counseling for Anxiety
by Elaine Leong Eng, MD

Offering a unique spiritual and mental health perspective on a major malady of our age, this practicing Christian psychiatrist has packed a dose of reality mixed with medicine and faith into a book aimed at informing, inspiring, and equipping those who wish to better help those who struggle with anxiety and related disorders, both inside and outside the church. As one endorser said, "I travel all over the world. I see fellow believers suffering from different forms of anxiety and worry. Dr. Eng's book gives me tools to recognize when people are suffering and how to encourage them to get the help they need."

Paperback: $19.99
eBook: $4.99

More books from the same author

Paperback: $14.99
eBook: $4.99

The Transforming Power of Story
Telling Your Story Brings Hope to Others and Healing to Yourself
by Elaine Leong Eng, MD & David B. Biebel, DMin

This book demonstrates, through multiple true life stories, how sharing one's story, especially in a group setting, can bring hope to listeners and healing to the one who shares. Individuals facing difficulties will find this book greatly encouraging.

Dr. Elaine Eng is a remarkable woman with an incredible story and personal ministry. She has been an inspiration to me for as long as I have known her. Her book will inspire you, bring tears of joy to your eyes, and longing to your heart, and reinforce your love for our wonderful Savior. Dr. Eng is a living, walking testimony to God's grace and power through human frailty. Her life and her stories show poignantly how He can use any circumstance for His glory.

Healthy Life Press
Books, eBooks, DVDs
Arvada, Colorado

A Small, Independent Christian Publisher with a big mission—to help people live healthier lives physically, emotionally, spiritually, and relationally.

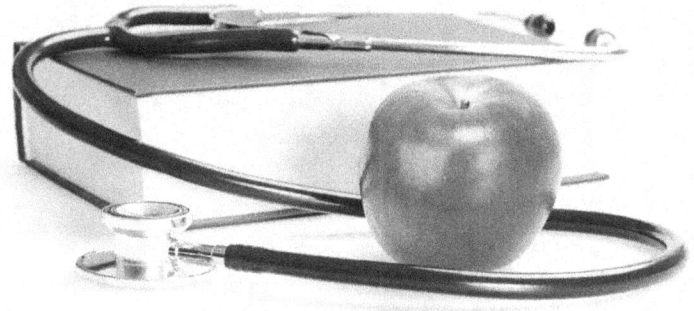

For a downloadable PDF catalog of our resources, and access to free sample excerpts from our books, visit: *www.healthylifepress.com*

1-877-331-2766 | *info@healthylifepress.com*

www.ingramcontent.com/pod-product-compliance
Lightning Source LLC
Chambersburg PA
CBHW071629080526
44588CB00010B/1338